Editor-in-Chief and Founder:
  *Lyndon H. LaRouche, Jr.*
Editorial Board: *Lyndon H. LaRouche, Jr. , Helga
  Zepp-LaRouche, Robert Ingraham, Tony
  Papert, Gerald Rose, Dennis Small, Jeffrey
  Steinberg, William Wertz*
Co-Editors: *Robert Ingraham, Tony Papert*
Technology: *Marsha Freeman*
Transcriptions: *Katherine Notley*
Ebooks: *Richard Burden*
Graphics: *Alan Yue*
Photos: *Stuart Lewis*
Circulation Manager: *Stanley Ezrol*

INTELLIGENCE DIRECTORS
Economics: *Marcia Merry Baker, Paul Gallagher*
History: *Anton Chaitkin*
Ibero-America: *Dennis Small*
Russia and Eastern Europe: *Rachel Douglas*
United States: *Debra Freeman*

INTERNATIONAL BUREAUS
Bogotá: *Miriam Redondo*
Berlin: *Rainer Apel*
Copenhagen: *Tom Gillesberg*
Lima: *Sara Madueño*
Melbourne: *Robert Barwick*
Mexico City: *Gerardo Castilleja Chávez*
New Delhi: *Ramtanu Maitra*
Paris: *Christine Bierre*
Stockholm: *Ulf Sandmark*
United Nations, N.Y.C.: *Leni Rubinstein*
Washington, D.C.: *William Jones*
Wiesbaden: *Göran Haglund*

ON THE WEB
e-mail: eirns@larouchepub.com
www.larouchepub.com
www.executiveintelligencereview.com
www.larouchepub.com/eiw
Webmaster: *John Sigerson*
Assistant Webmaster: *George Hollis*
Editor, Arabic-language edition: *Hussein Askary*

---

EIR (ISSN 0273-6314) *is published weekly
(50 issues), by EIR News Service, Inc.,
P.O. Box 17390, Washington, D.C. 20041-0390.
(703) 297-8434*

**European Headquarters:** E.I.R. GmbH, Postfach
Bahnstrasse 9a, D-65205, Wiesbaden, Germany
Tel: 49-611-73650
Homepage: http://www.eir.de
e-mail: info@eir.de
Director: Georg Neudecker

**Montreal, Canada:** 514-461-1557
eir@eircanada.ca

**Denmark:** EIR - Danmark, Sankt Knuds Vej 11,
basement left, DK-1903 Frederiksberg, Denmark.
Tel.: +45 35 43 60 40, Fax: +45 35 43 87 57. e-mail:
eirdk@hotmail.com.

**Mexico City:** EIR, Sor Juana Inés de la Cruz 242-2
Col. Agricultura C.P. 11360
Delegación M. Hidalgo, México D.F.
Tel. (5525) 5318-2301
eirmexico@gmail.com

Copyright: ©2018 EIR News Service. All rights
reserved. Reproduction in whole or in part without
permission strictly prohibited.

Canada Post Publication Sales Agreement
#40683579

**Postmaster:** Send all address changes to *EIR*, P.O.
Box 17390, Washington, D.C. 20041-0390.

Signed articles in *EIR* represent the views of the authors,
and not necessarily those of the Editorial Board.

# Now Only LaRouche's Methods Will Work

# June 12, 2018: The Spirit of the New Silk Road Shines in Its Full Glory

This day will be remembered in history, not only for the extraordinary achievement in Korea brought about by Donald Trump, Kim Jong-un, Moon Jae-in, Xi Jinping, Shinzo Abe, and Vladimir Putin, but because the "Spirit of the New Silk Road" has taken another giant step forward in bringing peace and development to the entire world.

The Joint Statement signed and released by Chairman Kim and President Trump is reproduced on page 3. It states clearly that the new relationship between the United States and the DPRK "will contribute to peace and prosperity of the Korean Peninsula and of the world."

In a press conference following the Summit, President Trump spoke profoundly about the transformation taking place in the world as a whole. He began: "I stand before you as a representative of the Unites States to deliver a message of hope and vision, and a message of peace." He said that the successful Summit proved that "real change is indeed possible;" that "the past does not have to define the future;" that "anyone can make war, but only the most courageous can make peace." He concluded, correctly, that "It's a very great moment in the history of the world."

It is being noted around the world that this historic event in Singapore, and the similarly transformational meeting of the Shanghai Cooperation Organization (SCO) which took place over the weekend in Qingdao, stand in stark contrast to the chaos at the G-7 meeting in Quebec, where Trump declared that Putin should be at the table if anything of use were to be accomplished. Trump received full backing from the newly elected Prime Minister of Italy Giuseppe Conte, while Shinzo Abe has also refused to join in the Russia-bashing, and is working closely with President Putin on joint development projects. What is left of the G-7—France, Germany, Canada and the U.K.—may end up being the G-4, if they fail to break from the British Empire's desperate effort to sustain the division of the world into East and West.

History is being made in Asia, not in the decrepit economies and cultural decay of the West. Trump's appreciation of China and Russia reflects his recognition that, working together, great changes can be made for the betterment of mankind as a whole, and that the United States itself can only be restored to its former greatness by being part of the Spirit of the New Silk Road, as Helga Zepp-LaRouche has described it. This Spirit is contagious, inspiring cultural optimism, and stands in stark contrast to the cultural pessimism which has increasingly infected Europe and the United States over the past fifty years.

Mrs. LaRouche, after watching Trump's Singapore press conference, noted that Trump had refused to be provoked by the hysterical, war-mongering western media, but rather showed total confidence that the new paradigm for peace through development were both possible and necessary. This is what Lyndon LaRouche and this movement have been fighting for over these past fifty years. It is a time of historical transformation, a phase-change in the topology of human development, in which the actions of a single individual can change the world. There should be no sitting on the fence. People should be told, boldly, to join with the LaRouche movement, to bring the Spirit of the New Silk Road to all of Mankind.

Joint Statement of President Donald J. Trump of the United States of America and
Chairman Kim Jong-Un of the Democratic Peoples Republic of Korea at the Singapore Summit

Issued on: June 12, 2018

President Donald J. Trump of the United States of America and Chairman Kim Jong-un of the State Affairs Commission of the Democratic Peoples Republic of Korea (DPRK) held a first, historic summit in Singapore on June 12, 2018.

President Trump and Chairman Kim Jong-un conducted a comprehensive, in-depth, and sincere exchange of opinions on the issues related to the establishment of new U.S.-DPRK relations and the building of a lasting and robust peace regime on the Korean Peninsula. President Trump committed to provide security guarantees to the DPRK, and Chairman Kim Jong-un reaffirmed his firm and unwavering commitment to complete denuclearization of the Korean Peninsula.

Convinced that the establishment of new U.S.-DPRK relations will contribute to the peace and prosperity of the Korean Peninsula and of the world, and recognizing that mutual confidence building can promote the denuclearization of the Korean Peninsula, President Trump and Chairman Kim Jong-un state the following:

1. The United States and the DPRK commit to establish new U.S.-DPRK relations in accordance with the desire of the peoples of the two countries for peace and prosperity.
2. The United States and the DPRK will join their efforts to build a lasting and stable peace regime on the Korean Peninsula.
3. Reaffirming the April 27, 2018 Panmunjom Declaration, the DPRK commits to work toward complete denuclearization of the Korean Peninsula.
4. The United States and the DPRK commit to recovering POW/MIA remains, including the immediate repatriation of those already identified.

Having acknowledged that the U.S.-DPRK summit—the first in history—was an epochal event of great significance in overcoming decades of tensions and hostilities between the two countries and for the opening up of a new future, President Trump and Chairman Kim Jong-un commit to implement the stipulations in this joint statement fully and expeditiously. The United States and the DPRK commit to hold follow-on negotiations, led by the U.S. Secretary of State, Mike Pompeo, and a relevant high-level DPRK official, at the earliest possible date, to implement the outcomes of the U.S.-DPRK summit.

President Donald J. Trump of the United States of America and Chairman Kim Jong-un of the State Affairs Commission of the Democratic Peoples Republic of Korea have committed to cooperate for the development of new U.S.-DPRK relations and for the promotion of peace, prosperity, and security of the Korean Peninsula and of the world.

DONALD J. TRUMP
President of the United States of America

KIM JONG-UN
Chairman of the State Affairs Commission of the Democratic Peoples Republic of Korea

June 12, 2018 Sentosa Island Singapore

# ΞIR Contents

www.larouchepub.com     Volume 45, Number 24, June 15, 2018

White House/Shealah Craighead

# I. Grant Us Peace, Through Economic Development

International Schiller Institute Conference
New York City, June 9, 2018

# 'Dona Nobis Pacem'

## Grant Us Peace, Through Economic Development

10:30-11:30 AM  REGISTRATION

11:30-12:00 noon

GREETINGS by Schiller Institute moderator Dennis Speed, including international messages

Violin Sonata in G minor, Adagio and Fugue, J.S. Bach
*Xinou Wei, Violinist*

12:00 noon-2:00 PM

**PANEL 1: A New Paradigm of Global Relations, Ending Geopolitics—the Four Powers**

KEYNOTE: *Helga Zepp-LaRouche, Founder and Chairwoman of the Schiller Institute*

**The New Silk Road Spirit Is Contagious**

Jason Ross, *coauthor, Schiller Institute Special Report, "Extending the New Silk Road to West Asia and Africa, A Vision of an Economic Renaissance"*

Dr. Xu Wenhong, *Deputy Secretary General of the Center for Belt and Road Studies, Chinese Academy of Social Sciences*

Dmitry Polyanskiy, *First Deputy Permanent Representative of the Russian Federation to the United Nations*

DISCUSSION

2:00-2:30 PM  BREAK

2:30-4:30 PM

**PANEL 2: Choosing Creativity—Not Tragedy— In Economics and Statecraft**

Dennis Speed, *Northeast Coordinator, Schiller Institute*
**The LaRouche Method: Seed-Crystal of a New Culture**

James George Jatras, *former U.S. Diplomat and former Adviser to the Republican Senate Leadership*
**The Urgency of a Trump-Putin Summit**

Richard Black, *Virginia State Senator*
**The Strategic Importance of Victory, Peace and Development in Syria**

DISCUSSION

# Message to 'Dona Nobis Pacem' New York Conference

*by Liliana Gorini, chairwoman of Movisol, the LaRouche Movement in Italy*

Dear members and friends of the Schiller Institute,

Recent events in Italy have just proven what poet and historian Friedrich Schiller has taught us, that "man is greater than his destiny." Last week our duly elected government, which had received 60% of the votes, was vetoed by the European Union and the European Central Bank (ECB), in Frankfurt, Germany, with an attempted coup, which failed. Their intention was to impose on Italy yet another technocratic government, led by IMF representative Carlo Cottarelli. But the Italian population reacted against this coup, and expressed their support for the government of Prof. Carlo Conte, and for the two parties which had won the elections on March 4: Lega and the Five Star Movement. The electorate demanded that decisions on our economic policy be taken in Italy, and not in Brussels or Frankfurt.

The government of Professor Conte, which had been vetoed by the ECB, was sworn in on June 1, and won a vote of confidence at the Parliament two days ago. It is the first government in the world which includes two points dear to LaRouche in its official program: Glass-Steagall and national banking; its Economics Minister Tria is in favor of the Belt and Road Initiative, speaks Chinese, and spoke in favor of public investments in infrastructure, confirming that the spirit of the New Paradigm is alive and well in Italy.

And that may be the reason why the financial oligarchy, and the City of London, were fully mobilized to stop this government, and called it "barbaric" (in the *Financial Times*).

Conte's request to review sanctions against Russia has a lot of support from small- and medium-sized companies which suffered the consequences of such sanctions, but opposition was immediately unleashed against it by NATO head Jens Stoltenberg and German Chancellor Angela Merkel: They threatened Italy with the Greece treatment. However, Conte found an ally in President Trump at the G-7 in Canada, where both called for Russia to be included again.

Movisol has been fighting for years for LaRouche's Four Laws, and over the last two years, collected 198 signatures of members of Parliament, economists, and other VIPs, on a petition to President Trump, asking him to keep his promise and reinstate Glass-Steagall, which would not only "make America great, but the whole world."

Four ministers of the new Italian government are among the signers of our petition. We can change the world, and we can be greater than our destiny.

I wish you all the best for this important conference on peace through development, *Dona nobis pacem*.

# Greeting

*From Ali Alghaffari, 9th Grade, 14 years old, Yemen*

I, Ali, on behalf of my colleagues in the Modern Language School in Sana'a, am sorry to send these lines while some schools in the United States are facing violence and gun shots!

It is strange that we in Sana'a are under the worst Joint UK-United States-Saudi coalition attack, and despite their killing of numbers of us on a daily basis, and shooting at our schools with rockets, we have never had a situation where we kill each other in our schools or towns!

We think that you and we have both suffered a lot, not in accordance with the laws of the universe, and it's time to leave those that would control our destiny and break our dignity, and head to a shared future that overcomes the real reasons behind school and home violence!

It is not beyond reach that Students can change the game, and here we are in Yemen. I couldn't join you due to the Airport blockade that has been in place for a year in our capital, but I am sharing here our dream alongside the spirit that has been gifted to us by Mrs. Helga LaRouche, the Founder of the Schiller Institutes, which has paved many roads for us in Yemen to link our freedom to the New Silk Road, and which unites all of us today.

The power of Humanity didn't always show in our community, hence you can see that our Modern Language School has adopted from across the oceans the Physical Economic principles of LaRouche via our Silk Road School program. We study that in a manual and in a class we take to understand how to end poverty, and to achieve the Sustainable Development

Goals of 2030.

Finally, I invite you to learn about our famous Yemeni Happy Miracle report that is designed to link us with the Belt and Road Initiative. This report gives significant attention to students, and I have a photo in the report. The report was launched at my birthday celebration, attended by all the champions for the Belt and Road Initiative in Yemen.

## Max Lu
*Chairman, United Nations World Silk Road Forum (UNWSF)*

To the international think tank Schiller Institute and to the Institute's Chairman:

I understand that the Schiller Institute will soon hold the second event in the United States aimed at promoting the "Belt and Road Initiative" for young Americans on the 8th of June, and an international conference the following day in New York City. On behalf of myself and the United Nations World Silk Road Forum, I would like to express my sincere congratulations on the hosting of this promotional campaign, and wish the conference a complete success.

The "Belt and Road Initiative" is based on the principles of "world consultation, joint contribution and shared benefits" and "political mutual trust, economic integration, and cultural inclusion." It is based on "policy communication, facilities connectivity, unimpeded trade, capital financing, and people-mindedness." This great initiative of China aims to build a "human centered community." The resolution written by the United Nations General Assembly and the Security Council has been recognized and actively participated in by the international community over the past five years. All countries and people participating in the "Belt and Road Initiative" have benefited greatly.

As a non-profit and non-governmental organization, the World Silk Road Forum of the United Nations has played a prominent role at the United Nations over the past two years. With its vision of globalization, it has fully implemented the "One Belt and One Road" initiative, and has been continuously active on the civilian level, actively promoting and publicizing the "Belt and Road Initiative" and building bridges and ties for international cooperation among companies and civic organizations in various countries. We are willing to cooperate with the Schiller Institute and work together to do a good job in promoting and putting into practice the "Belt and Road Initiative."

Finally, I wish the international think tank, the Schiller Institute, great accomplishments, and I wish you, Chairman, good health and successful efforts.

June 4, 2018

THE PAST SPEAKS TO THE FUTURE
# RFK's Message in South Africa, and the Call for Global Revolutionary Change

*This is the message sent by Ramasimong Phillip Tsokolibane, leader of LaRouche South Africa, to the Schiller Institute conference in New York City, "Dona Nobis Pacem," held June 9, 2018.*

On behalf of my nation, South Africa, proud member of the BRICS alliance for peace and development and the host of the BRICS summit next month, I send greetings to you who are gathered in New York City under the auspices of the Schiller Institute to discuss and organize the fight for the New Global Paradigm.

While we can see the progress being made in that direction, I urge you to double your efforts, as we have yet to secure victory against a dirty and determined, British Imperial elite and their assets around the globe, who will not yield their power over international finance, and with it, their ability to slaughter and subjugate much of humanity. They cannot win, but the world can lose, as they continue to light the flames of discord and war, to topple governments, including their attempt to topple the government of President Trump in the United States, and to promote confrontation with the leading standard bearers of the New Paradigm, Russia and China.

For the sake of Africa—whose populations the racist leadership of the British Empire seek to eliminate—and for the rest of the world, I say, "Do not yet declare victory, even as that victory is in sight." As the



Now Only LaRouche's Methods Will Work    7

LaRouches, Lyn and Helga, have repeatedly instructed, the change we seek is revolutionary, one that throws off the entire monetarist system of the Empire of Money, and replaces it with a system that understands that only creative human labor—physical and mental—can produce wealth, a system that insists on investing in that which increases the productivity of human labor. The creation of money-valued "wealth" is not our objective; our objective is to increase the number of creative human beings living on this planet, to drive progress everywhere.

The brutish, British-run system—the old paradigm—cannot be reformed; its problems are not structural, but are derived from its anti-human monetarist principles that use calculations of the cost of maintaining human lives as a justification for genocide. Such calculations—"bankers' arithmetic"—have turned nations, and continents such as Africa, in the recent past into death-dealing cauldrons. Only now, through policies promoted by the BRICS, and China's Belt and Road Initiative (BRI) do we see this changing.

Only the foolish, or those professional liars who work for the dying Empire and its media sewers, could imagine that these two divergent views of Humankind could coexist. The Empire's system *must* die, because it has reached the limits of its self-cannibalization. But unless we throw it off, its death agony can kill us all.

So the burning question of the day is how to build a movement for revolutionary change that can bring the world to embrace, and that quickly, the policies and principles of the New Paradigm.

I believe a speech given by Robert Francis Kennedy in South Africa, on June 6, 1966—two years to the day before his assassination at British instigation in as yet unclear circumstances—provides us with some insight into how this can be done. As did Lyndon LaRouche, in the founding of the movement for which I am the spokesman in South Africa, RFK insisted that revolutions are organized not by amorphous masses of angry people, but by initiatives of individual personalities, alone and in concert with each other.

In discussing this in the context of resistance to the evil, British Empire–inspired Apartheid system in South Africa, as well as the civil rights struggle in the United States, Robert Kennedy said that change is not brought about through violence of unthinking mobs or individuals, but through the spread of ideas that cause a creative challenge to the old order. He stressed that it is the responsibility of the younger generation to lead the way to change, against the resistance of older generations who might cling, unnecessarily, to the failed ways of the old paradigm.

But let Kennedy himself speak directly to us today, from the past.

First let us set the stage for his remarks.

He had been invited to South Africa by Ian Robertson, the president of the National Union of South African Students, to speak at their annual Day of Reaffirmation of Academic and Human Freedom. The apartheid-burdened South African government was hesitant to let Kennedy speak, but eventually granted him a visa for fear of snubbing a future President of the United States.

Two weeks before the scheduled event, Robertson himself was banned by the government from participating in social and political life for five years, and so was unable to attend. An empty chair marked his absence. Visas were denied to 40 news correspondents that were to cover the event. A crowd of 18,000 white students and faculty packed the hall in Cape Town. Banners hung in protest of the Vietnam War. Following a ceremonial procession, led by a student carrying an extinguished "torch of academic freedom," Kennedy made his entrance.

When he finally had the audience's close and silent attention, he opened by employing ironic misdirection. He said:

> I come here this evening because of my deep interest and affection for a land settled by the Dutch in the mid-seventeenth century, then taken over by the British, and at last independent; a land in which the native inhabitants were at first subdued, but relations with whom remain a problem to this day; a land which defined itself on a hostile frontier; a land which has tamed rich natural resources through the energetic application of modern technology; a land which was once the importer of slaves, and now must struggle to wipe out the last traces of that former bondage. I refer, of course, to the United States of America.

This drew laughter and applause, and released the tension. After thanking the student union for the invitation, Kennedy discussed individual liberty, apartheid, communism, and the need for civil rights. He emphasized inclusiveness, individual action, and the importance of youth involvement in society. At the climax, he listed four "dangers" that would obstruct the goals of civil rights, equality, and justice. The first is futility, "the belief there is nothing one man or one woman can do against the enormous array of the world's ills." Kennedy countered:

> Yet many of the world's great movements, of thought and action, have flowed from the work of a single man. A young monk began the Protestant Reformation, a young general extended an empire from Macedonia to the borders of the earth, and a young woman reclaimed the territory of France. It was a young Italian explorer who discovered the New World, and 32-year-old Thomas Jefferson who proclaimed that all men are created equal. "Give me a place to stand," said Archimedes, "and I will move the world." These men moved the world, and so can we all....
>
> It is from numberless diverse acts of courage and belief that human history is shaped each time a man stands up for an ideal or acts to improve the lot of others or strikes out against injustice. He sends forth a tiny ripple of hope, and crossing each other from a million different centers of energy and daring, those ripples build a current that can sweep down the mightiest wall of oppression and resistance.

The second danger is expediency, the idea "that hopes and beliefs must bend before immediate necessities.... [T]here is no basic inconsistency between ideals and realistic possibilities—no separation between the deepest desires of heart and of mind and the rational application of human effort to human problems."

The third danger is timidity. "Moral courage is a rarer commodity than bravery in battle or great intelligence. Yet it is the one essential, vital quality for those who seek to change the world which yields most painfully to change."

The fourth and final danger, comfort: "The temptation to follow the easy and familiar path of personal ambition and financial success so grandly spread before those who have the privilege of an education." But comfort is not really an option:

> [Comfort] is not the road history has marked out

for us. There is a Chinese curse which says, "May he live in interesting times." Like it or not, we live in interesting times. They are times of danger and uncertainty; but they are also the most creative of any time in the history of mankind. And everyone here will ultimately be judged—will ultimately judge himself—on the effort he has contributed to building a new world society and the extent to which his ideals and goals have shaped that effort.

I suggest to you that Robert Kennedy's voice speaks great truths across history to us—we who must organize a global movement of individuals for revolutionary change. He tells us that we must reject expediency, pragmatism and easy answers. I would add that these are often offered by British agents and provocateurs, often on the payrolls of organizations affiliated with the pro-Nazi financier, George Soros.

We must also stay focused on the "big picture." It is a *global* change that must be organized. We must never let ourselves hide in some local or even national fight that takes us away from our objective.

And, we also must accept that it will be those who are young in both spirit and mind, and embrace change, who must carry the greatest burden and responsibility for realizing the change we seek. The change we seek is not "change for the sake of change" of the London-run, rock-drug-sex counterculture which, after the assassinations of the Kennedys and Dr. Martin Luther King, Jr, led so many down so many counterproductive back alleys and dead endings. Ours is a fight for a principled change, which the LaRouches have led for the last 50 years.

Robert Kennedy believed that with proper leadership, such change can take place. So do I.

He concluded his Reaffirmation address in Cape Town by quoting his slain brother, President John Kennedy, in his inaugural address. So will I:

> The energy, the faith, the devotion which we bring to this endeavor will light our country and all who serve it—and the glow from that fire can truly light the world.... With a good conscience our only sure reward, with history the final judge of our deeds, let us go forth and lead the land we love, asking His blessing and His help, but knowing that here on earth God's work must truly be our own.

# A New Paradigm of Global Relations, Ending Geopolitics—The Four Powers

ZEPP-LAROUCHE

# Schiller Institute Conference Keynote: The New Silk Road Spirit Is Contagious

*Helga Zepp-LaRouche, founder of the Schiller Institutes, gave this keynote address to the Schiller Institute conference, "Dona Nobis Pacem—Grant Us Peace, Through Economic Development," convened in New York City on Saturday, June 9, 2018. Her keynote opened Panel 1 of the conference.*

**Dennis Speed:** The idea of this conference is expressed in the graphic that was created for the concert that will follow the conference tomorrow. It features Martin Luther King, Jr., Robert Kennedy, and Ludwig van Beethoven. Choosing creativity as opposed to tragedy has been the hallmark of the Schiller Institute as it was created by the woman who you are about to hear.

Back in 1984, when it appeared that the world was also on a tragic course to war, this institution was proposed to the United States. But the United States rejected it, and the founder of this organization then independently created it in collaboration with her husband, Lyndon LaRouche. Many of us were privileged to be part of that when it began. The idea of this organization, the Schiller Institute, is to change thinking; change the method by which people deliberate on policy. As Lyndon LaRouche once stated in a document he wrote, "The content of policy is the method by which it is made," and that means the conceptual method by which it is made.

We find ourselves today in a very interesting situa-

Schiller Institute

*Helga Zepp-LaRouche, founder of the Schiller Institutes.*

tion internationally, and you're going to hear all about that. But I just want to say in introducing the woman who founded this organization, that throughout the world now, we find the conceptions and the seed crystal of the conceptions that she recognized and fought for: the need to uplift, in the form of talking about a cultural paradigm shift; that you couldn't simply have a set of programs or policies, you had to have a new set of individuals.

The conception that we want to give you of what we are trying to do here today, is that you also are part of that New Paradigm, and how you think and how your thinking changes, together with many other people from around the world who are part of these deliberations, is really the subject of how the changes that we're seeing right now all over the world are going to be effected.

Our first panel, "A New Paradigm of Global Relations: Ending Geopolitics," is an idea that, particularly since 2013 in the case of New York City, we've been doing forums around. We tried to force the situation to happen, and we now have that possibility, including the Presidency of the United States, being integrated into that with Russia, China, and India. So, to tell us how Earth's next fifty years and how this policy of a new cultural paradigm and an ending of geopolitics can happen, we're presenting the founder of the Schiller Institute, Helga Zepp-LaRouche.

*Vladimir Putin, Russian President (left) with Alexander Van der Bellen, Federal President of the Republic of Austria, Vienna, June 5, 2016.*



**Helga Zepp-LaRouche:** Thank you. Ladies and gentlemen, dear friends of the Schiller Institute, I'm actually very optimistic about the situation. I think there is the absolute possibility that we will, in the very near term, see the emergence of a completely New Paradigm of civilization. Because a majority of nations are gathering around the idea that there is only one humanity which is of a higher order than national interests and even geopolitical confrontation. Never before has the contradiction and the openness of the fight between the New Paradigm and the old paradigm been more obvious than right now. This conference was originally planned to speed this process up and to urge in particular a summit as early as possible between President Trump and President Putin, as the only way to outflank the ongoing British-initiated and -conducted coup against the United States, by simply shifting the level of the discussion to the the two Presidents directly.

There is great hope that such a summit will take place in the near future. There is talk that it could take place in July. This was initiated when President Putin just concluded what I would say is an historic visit to Austria, where it was proposed that Austria, as a neutral country and as a country which very consciously understands itself as a bridge between East and West, be the venue of such a conference. President Putin just expressed today that he is looking forward to it very much and thinks it would be a very productive event.

Now, the important changes which are taking place are best illustrated by the two parallel conferences and summits that are taking place this weekend; one, the G-7, taking place in Canada; and the other, the SCO, the Shanghai Cooperation Organization, meeting, in Qingdao, China. At the G-7, most of the countries, or at least some of them, want to defend the status quo of the neo-liberal, geopolitical old paradigm; and at the Shanghai Cooperation Organization, the attending nations are trying to establish a new order—a win-win cooperation of all nations on this planet.

On the G-7 meeting: Trump arrived late and he's leaving early, he refused to meet the Prime Minister of Great Britain, Theresa May—which I think is a good thing—in order to go quickly on to Singapore to have his summit with North Korea's leader Kim Jong-un. Trump made his concern clear, saying that he thought the grouping of people at this G-7 summit was not the right combination because Russia was not there, and that the G-8 should be reconstituted. President Trump stated that this may not be politically correct, but after all we have a world to run.

I think that that is exactly the right spirit. You could

*President Donald Trump with other G-7 leaders in summit talks, Charlevoix, Canada, June 8-9, 2018.*

see the disunity in French President Macron and Canadian Prime Minister Trudeau getting into a fuss with Trump beforehand, even saying if the tensions with Trump on the trade escalate, the G-7 will become only a G-6+1. But then something very interesting happened, namely that the new Prime Minister of Italy, Giuseppe Conte, backed up Trump's demand that the group should return to a G-8; so maybe it's now only the G5, after all. What Conte did there is a very clear break in the unity of the European Union.

The problem with the European establishments is that they completely resist learning. They don't learn from or understand the increasing failure of their model of the world order—which they developed after the collapse of the Soviet Union. This is a model based establishing a unipolar world to which all countries must submit—those nations that do not want to do submit get regime changed through color revolution or so-called humanitarian intervention wars, as happened in Iraq, in Libya, as was attempted in Syria, and as is ongoing in the Ukraine. Part of that world order idea was also to encircle Russia and China, ultimately imposing regime change in those two countries, to get rid of President Putin and to get rid of the Communist leadership of China—as unlikely a proposition as that might be.

Another part of that collapsing world order is the neo-liberal system which went for the complete deregulation of the financial system, which increased the gap between the rich and the poor. What we have been seeing now is a revolt, actually on a global scale against that neo-liberal dying old system of the British Empire. It was expressed through the Brexit vote; it was expressed through the election of President Trump and defeat of Hillary Clinton; it was expressed in the vote against the change of the Constitution in Italy last year; it was becoming clear in the election of the present Austrian government; and now, of the new Italian government.

Something very noteworthy just happened in Italy, which I think it is important for the whole world to understand; because it is a reflection of why the European model does not function. The two parties which were

Palazzo del Quirinale

*Sergio Mattarella (center), the Italian President who rejected Paolo Savona as Economy and Finance Minister, under pressure from the British-directed European Union bureaucracy.*

CC/Filippo Viliani

*Paolo Savona*

just elected—the Lega and the Five Star Movement—were so-called "euro-critical" parties which were expressing the same absolute discontent with the neo-liberal paradigm as expressed in the election of President Trump, the Brexit vote, and the Austrian election.

That a euro-critical government would come into power in Italy caused a big uproar in Brussels, the de facto capital of the European Union. EU Commissioner Oettinger, who is quite a character, said openly "The markets will teach the Italians how to vote." That is not exactly in the spirit of democracy, but here you have it. Following Oettinger's remarks, the European Central Bank, as reported by the *Financial Times*, started to enable the speculators to speculate against the Italian state bonds by reducing the amount of state bonds they had been buying on a monthly basis, and therefore causing the so-called spread to increase to up to 300 points with respect to German bonds. That was the pressure which was then used by Italy's President Sergio Mattarella to refuse the first proposal for Giuseppe Conte to become the new Prime Minister.

Mattarella gave a speech which is really noteworthy, because he said that the foreign investors don't like the proposed Finance Minister Savona; because he is known to be critical of the euro, and wants to reform the Eurozone system. Mattarella refused Savona. Savona is an establishment economist; he was the head of the industrial association in Italy; he had been a minister in a previous moderate government. He was pro-euro in the beginning, but only after he realized the consequences of the Maastricht Stability Pact of austerity imposed on Italy by Brussels, that it totally ruined the Italian economy, that he became critical and demanded that Italy should develop a Plan B in case that it would not work and conditions for the Italian people did not improve. He demanded that the Maastricht rules be renegotiated.

## Merkel Values: Warships to South China Sea

Angela Merkel, the German Chancellor, earlier had said, "Yes, we have a democracy, but it is a democracy in conformity with the markets." Now, this Italian case where the President bends under pressure from the ECB [European Central Bank] and the European Union to refuse a prime minister candidate proposed by those parties which have just won the majority, is really an absolute scandal. It means that democracy does not exist. I think it's a very severe development, because it shows you where we are really in terms of the famous "Western values" which they always are talking about. The head of the Italian metal trade union made a noteworthy comment. He said that the fact that an establishment person like Savona is being regarded as subversive, shows you how much to the right the European Union has moved in the last decades under the rule of neo-liberal policies. That is exactly the problem.

Obviously this tactic failed; it boomeranged. The effort to impose a technocratic prime minister also did not work. Now, you have the same Giuseppe Conte as Prime Minister of Italy. In his inaugural speech to the Italian parliament, among other things he said, "We will support opening up to Russia … We will push for a review of the sanctions system, starting with those that risk humiliating Russian civil society." That sentiment was echoed by Chancellor Sebastian Kurz from Austria, who will chair the European Union beginning the 1st of July. Conte promised that he will, step by step, move to reduce the sanctions and actually get out of the sanctions regime all together. He also announced that there will be a big investment program to recover the industrial development of Italy.

Let's look at this. European unity is only wishful thinking of people suffering from European group-think. Look at the condition of Europe: the Visegrad countries—that is, Poland, the Czech Republic, Hungary, and Slovakia; the Eastern and Central European countries—all want better relations with China, and most of them with Russia. The same goes for the Balkans states; it goes for Southern Europe—for Greece, for Italy, for Spain and Portugal—all want to be hubs of the New Silk Road policy.

So, there is no unity. Brussels, on the other hand, is insisting on a system which is a super bureaucratic huge apparatus; Mrs. Merkel demands that Germany and Europe take fate into their own hands. German Foreign Minister Maas is demanding that Europe form new alliances. The question is, what countries do Merkel and Maas want to form new alliances with, since they are against Russia? Merkel just opposed Russia being brought back into the G-8. In fact, Russia doesn't even want to be in the G-8; why join such an obsolete grouping? Brussels and Germany are also trying to block the influence of China's New Silk Road, so where would new alliances come from?

Germany is sending, for the first time, military forces to maneuvers in the South China Sea, where German ships, with French soldiers onboard, will violate the territorial waters of Chinese islands. What is this? What is this idea of Europe playing a new imperial, global role, as German Defense Minister von der Leyen is promoting all the time? This is an old model. I do not expect any positive changes to come from the core countries who want to defend the status quo. I do expect a lot of positive changes to come from those countries in Europe who want to cooperate with the New Silk Road.

## News from Asia

Contrast the condition of Europe at this point with what is going on in Asia. It could not be more dramatic. You have a new model of win-win cooperation, of acting in the interest of the other, of respect of the sovereignty of the other country, of non-interference, of respect for the different social system of the other country, and of the idea to be united for a higher purpose of the one mankind. That policy, the result of China's New Silk Road policy on the table for almost five years, has developed the most incredible dynamic ever. It is already become the largest infrastructure project in history, and it is clear it will define the new rules of the world.

Let's look at these new rules. At the core of the new strategic realignment going on in the world, is the comprehensive strategic partnership between Russia and China, cemented by a very deep personal friendship between President Putin and President Xi Jinping. Putin, who just made a state visit to China before his appearance at the SCO meeting, was awarded the Friendship Medal of China in a big celebration in the Great Hall of the People at Tiananmen Square.

Putin just conducted his annual question and answer session with the Russian people. He answered eighty-seven questions, taking somewhere between six and eight hours to do so—an extensive dialogue with the Russian people. Russian media reported that 91.3% of Russians think that wisdom is the most important trait of President Putin. Obviously, he has a tremendous charisma. People also voted on what would be their dream encounter with Putin: 37.8% want to have their picture taken with Putin; 29.9% would like to get a puppy from this dog-loving President—I would choose that option, naturally; and 22.47% want a big hug from their President.

I'm telling you all this because I know it's upsetting to those who are used to the demonizing of Putin by the mainstream media. I can assure you that this admiration for Putin does not only exist in Russia; it also exists in China. There was just an article in the Chinese media reporting that the reason why tens of millions of Chinese—actually more than ten million—have formed a Putin fan club on the Internet. They said the reason for the Chinese friendly attitude towards Putin is that they share a disgust for the arrogance of the West. The Chinese people note that the treatment of Putin and Presi-

*Narendra Modi, Prime Minister of India, delivering keynote address at Shangri-La Dialogue, Singapore, June 1, 2018.*

dent Xi by the West is the same: demonizing, slandering. Actually, it is the same against President Trump concerning the way he is treated by the neo-liberal mainstream media.

But there are also other Asian countries that are affected by the New Silk Road Spirit. During the Obama administration, the policy of the United States was the "Asia pivot"; which was nothing but a geopolitical manipulation of the India-Pacific countries—Australia, Japan, New Zealand, and India—to form an India-Pacific bulwark against China. The argument was to have India, the so-called "world's largest democracy," lining up with the Western democracies against the authoritarian China. That is no longer the case.

There was recently a two-day summit in Wuhan in China, where Prime Minister Modi and President Xi Jinping, in six sessions over two full days, discussing all kinds of bilateral and multilateral issues, contributing to a reset of the Indian policy towards China. Modi just gave a very important speech in Singapore at the Shangri-La Dialogue, where he outlined a completely different conception and made an appeal to the world to rise above competitiveness, and to work together in unity. He made several references to the Vedanta philosophy and the Vedas and the Upanishads. Modi said that the essential idea of the oneness of all is the basis of the new alliances in Asia:

"Asia and the world will be having a better future if India and China work together in trust and confidence, sensitive to each other's interests. This world is at a crossroad. There are both the temptations to repeat the worst lessons of history. But there is also the path of wisdom. It summons us to a higher purpose: To rise

*President Donald Trump (right) and Prime Minister Shinzo Abe of Japan confer at the United Nations General Assembly, Oct. 2, 2017.*

above the narrow view of our interests and recognize that each of us can serve our interests better when we work together as equals in the larger good of all nations. I am here to urge you to take that path. No other relationship of India's has as many layers as our relationship with China. I firmly believe that Asia and the world will have a better future if India and China work together with trust and confidence, keeping in mind each other's Interests."

India and China are now moving together, not apart. There is also a change in Japan in its relationship to Russia. While previously, Japan was pretty much of the Washington Consensus, in the recent period a complete change has occurred in the attitude of Prime Minister Shinzo Abe toward Russia. Russia and Japan are now working together in the economic development of the Kuril Islands, and Abe hopes, while he is still in office, to be able to sign a peace treaty with Russia, finally bringing to an end the technical state of war which still exists between Japan and Russia since World War II.

In the beginning, Japan was skeptical of China's Belt and Road Initiative. But then Abe sent Toshihiro Nikai, the Secretary General of the ruling Liberal Democratic Party, to the May 14-15, 2017 Belt and Road Forum in Beijing. Nikai is the second most important political person in Japan. From June 2017 onwards, Japan has been fully cooperating with China on the Belt and Road Initiative. Abe was the first foreign leader to visit President-elect Trump in Trump Tower on November 17, 2016; and he was the first foreign leader to meet Trump in the White House and then at Mar-a-Lago on February

10, 2017. This is also a new alliance emerging.

Then, if you look at the relationship between China and the United States, Xi Jinping visited President Trump in Mar-a-Lago last April. They developed an outstanding personal friendship. Xi Jinping returned that invitation by giving an extraordinary tour in the Forbidden City for President Trump and his wife. They named it a "state visit-plus." Now, you have now an alliance between all these major nations happening. Putin just commented on the prospective summit with Trump, saying the ball is in our court; let's make it work.

The world looks full of big expectations for next Tuesday, when the summit between President Trump and Kim Jong-un is to occur. I don't know if there will the big surprise, everything solved in one day—I don't think so. I think probably Russia Foreign Minister Lavrov is more right when he said that it will require a very skillful orchestration of reducing the sanctions and moving towards denuclearization in a step-by-step fashion in such a way that the security interests of North Korea are being taken care of, and that the promise that was made by Russia, that Russia will play a big role in the economic development of North Korea, and of President Trump who said that North Korea going on this path will become a very prosperous country, that this will all actually happen.

I think this situation would not be possible without the New Silk Road Spirit, which clearly has captured the imagination of the people of both North Korea and South Korea, who are all looking forward very much to developments which promise a reunification of the two Koreas. To have railway connections from the large port city of Busan in South Korea all the way to the Trans-Siberian Railway to connect to the Chinese railway! I think this is a very hopeful situation which can become the model to resolve all conflicts around the world.

## The Power of Creative Mind

This is actually the vision of my husband, Lyndon LaRouche, who already in 2007 demanded that the three countries—Russia, China, and India—absolutely must work together to counter the evil influence of the British Empire as it existed at that time. In 2009, at the Rhodes Forum of the Dialogue of Civilizations, my husband and

I made clear that the only way the world could get out of its present condition would be a four-power agreement among the United States, Russia, China, and India. Many Asians are now convinced that this coming century will be the Asian Century. It is very clear that the economic and scientific momentum is in Asia. If scientists want to do something important, they go to China; they go to other Asian countries. The economic growth rates of China and India and some other countries are far, far beyond anything in the so-called West.

But this is not sufficient. If we want to have something like what Xi Jinping calls the "community for a shared future for all of mankind," we need a cultural renaissance of the best traditions of all nations and cultures. The New Silk Road must be built on the most fundamental ontological, epistemological and metaphysical conceptions of all traditions. For China, this means the Confucian principle of self-perfection and life-long learning, and ennoblement of the character; of harmony in the midst of differences. For India, this means the Vedic concept about how the cosmic order must give the rules for the political life on Earth. The concept of the *dharma* for the Belt and Road Initiative; the concept of the Panchsheel Treaty; the concept of *ahimsa*, of developing your own character up to the point where you are unable to think any harmful thoughts.

European civilization, of which America is a part, has a lot to contribute in terms of its own humanist traditions. One of the most important conceptions of the new thinking was introduced by Nicholas of Cusa in the 15th Century—the *coincidentia oppositorum*: the coincidence of opposites, which means that human creativity and the human mind are able to create a higher order in which all differences vanish; the idea that order in the macrocosm can only exist if there is the maximum development of all microcosms, which means that all nations must develop in the maximum way, and act in the interests of each other in order to have a harmonious world.

The new thinking is expressed in the principles of the Peace of Westphalia: that in order to overcome war forever, foreign policy must be based on love and on the interest of the other. The new thinking must also be based on the ideas of Leibniz: that it is in the nature of the human character and in the character of the universe that evil can always be overcome with a greater

*Vladimir Vernadsky (shown in 1940), Russian biogeochemist who defined the concepts of the biosphere and the nöosphere.*

good: the ideas of Friedrich Schiller that each human being can be a beautiful soul for whom duty and passion, necessity and freedom, are one. The only people for whom this applies, however, are the geniuses. But the number of geniuses in the world will absolutely increase.

These are also the ideas of Vladimir Vernadsky, the Russian scientist, of whom my husband Lyndon LaRouche wrote in 2005 in his beautiful book, *Earth's Next Fifty Years.* In that book, he said that for Eurasian integration to work, it must be based on the ideas of Vladimir Vernadsky. That is, the influence of the nöosphere over the biosphere is continuously increasing, in other words, the results of the creative mind become more dominant in terms of the character of humanity. That is actually what we see happening with this development right now.

## Expose Spygate!

This is the spirit of a completely new era of mankind. This is beautiful, and it is happening. So, why are people not joining? Is it not a better model? Is it not obviously more fitting of human nature that we be united for higher goals and the common aims of mankind for the future? European civilization and part of the United States, moved away from their best European traditions; moved away from humanism.

The present dominant old paradigm model is based on neo-liberal and left-liberal ideas which can be traced directly back to the Frankfurt School and their so-called critical method. I don't have time now to discuss this in depth, but I can assure you I have looked at this in the past in much detail, and this is a completely destructive idea. It is the idea that you cannot have anything beautiful, truthful, that you cannot have a definite criteria for morality; but that everything can be put into question, and that anybody who claims that he has a way to know the truth in a scientific manner, or that you can define with scientific precision what is beauty, is a so-called "authoritarian" character.

Just recently, a big study came out from a big German think tank called Mercator Research Institute for China Studies (MERICS), attacking China's Belt and Road Initiative as an authoritarian model. It should be obvious to everyone, however, that what China is doing is based on the effort to establish truth, the effort to establish the common good for the people, and to make the world more beautiful. This has been stated repeatedly by Xi Jinping, for example at the 19th National Congress of the CPC [Communist Party of China], and at other recent events. I have come to the conclusion that that is also what is really inspiring President Putin and many other leaders of the developing countries.

The old geopolitical thinking has degenerated to the point that in terms of values, its proponents have adopted the principle that everything goes, everything is allowed. Such "thinking" has led to the present deep cultural crisis in the West; in America, the drug epidemics; the fact that the life expectancy is dropping in all age brackets, while the healthy life bracket in China for the first time is above that of the United States.

We need a cultural renaissance, and part of the reason we have this concert tomorrow is because it will give you a sense of the New Paradigm; what we absolutely have to accomplish in the tradition of the most beautiful accomplishments of European Classical traditions. If the Presidents—Trump, Putin, Prime Minister Modi, Xi Jinping—together with leaders of other developing countries and also hopefully some European countries, get together on these new ideas, this will mean the end of geopolitics, and therefore, the end of the causes of war as we have known them.

A big question being asked around the world is, "Can President Trump prevail, in light of the coup against him, in light of the influence of what people mistakenly call the "Deep State"—the military-industrial complex; and something that would be better called just plainly the British Empire? Are these forces too powerful to overwhelm President Trump? One has to understand the role of the British Empire, against which after all, the American Revolution was fought in the War of Independence. We have published a lot about the two-centuries-long efforts to undermine and subvert the American model of the republic.

Up until the election of Trump, the British Empire was extremely successful in corrupting the American establishment to adopt the model of the British Empire as their own; to rule the world on the basis of a unipolar world. We have seen that in the cases of the two Bush administrations, with the Obama administration, and in all the hysteria against Trump in Russiagate, initiated with the help or the initiation of the British secret services, because Trump is breaking with that tradition. This is the significance of Spygate. Remember, President Trump recently sent out a tweet saying, "SPYGATE could be one of the biggest political scandals in history!"

We have published several important reports which we are circulating, and you should help us to circulate internationally. Because if Spygate can be totally exposed, this will be the biggest catharsis you have ever seen, in which everything that has gone wrong in the last more than fifty years, since the assassinations of John F. Kennedy, of Robert Kennedy in 1968, and Martin Luther King, Jr.; the half-century of humiliation will be overcome and concluded, and must be replaced with the best tradition of the American culture and the American Revolution.

So, I'm asking you to join with the Schiller Institute to get exactly that accomplished. America must join with the New Silk Road, and we have to together create a New Paradigm for all of mankind. Thank you.

JASON ROSS

# Paradigms Collide:
# The Belt and Road Initiative in Africa

*Jason Ross is a member of Lyndon LaRouche's "Basement" science team in Purcellville, Virginia. This is a summary of his address to the Schiller Institute conference, "Dona Nobis Pacem— Grant Us Peace, Through Economic Development," convened in New York City on Saturday, June 9, 2018. He spoke on Panel 1 of the conference: "A New Paradigm of Global Relations, Ending Geopolitics—The Four Powers."*

Schiller Institute

*Jason Ross*

Jason Ross used the continent of Africa as a case study to understand the differences between the old, failing trans-Atlantic system and the new paradigm that China's Belt and Road Initiative (BRI) is making possible. The highest goal of a society or government is to afford its citizens efficient access, while they are alive, to the knowledge that their lives will have durable, immortal value to the future of humanity. China's adoption of the BRI as policy provides an increased potential for the United States to complete its historical mission of defeating the British Empire totally.

After briefly covering the imperial approaches towards Africa represented by the British (and by the United States itself under such policies as NSSM 200), Ross asked the audience what they thought about appeals made by aid and charitable agencies for the construction of wells and donations of goats to villages and families. Such assistance may appear to be a good thing. But we often use the word "good" to mean "better" than something else. Compared to having no water, a donated well for a village is "better." But if you live in a nation that is contributing to financial policies that prevent development, donating a well is *not* a good thing. Compared to opening the potential for full development, a well is a *bad* thing; it comes from an outlook that Africa will always be poor.

China has lifted 700 million people out of poverty over the past three decades. This was emphatically *not* accomplished by aid or charity provided by the other half-billion Chinese. It was accomplished through the intensive development of a higher platform of infrastructure, enabling a higher level of economic activity.

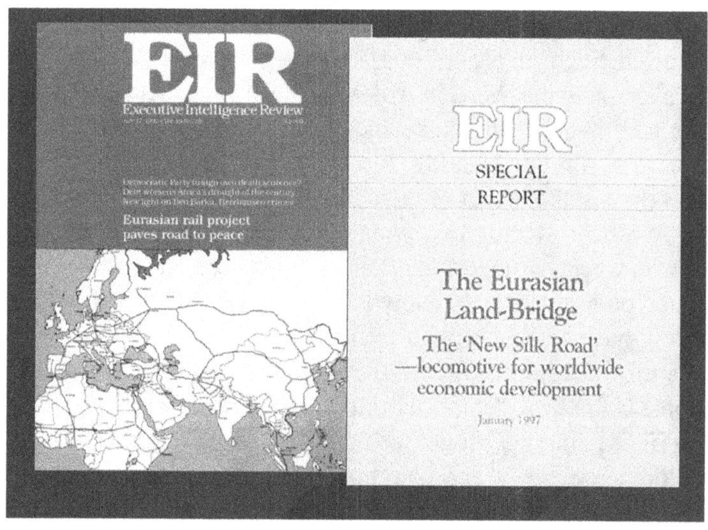

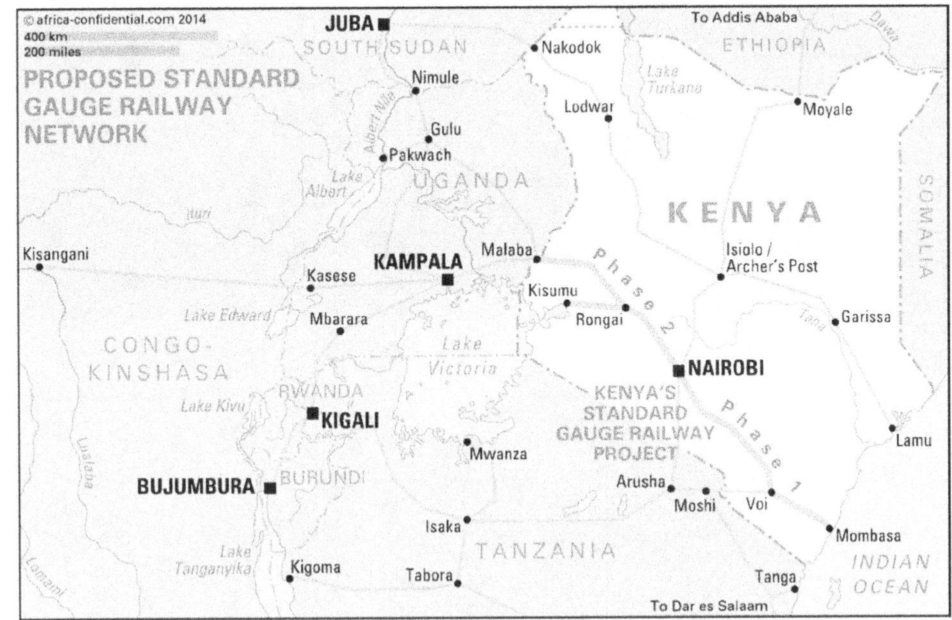



rail breakthroughs in Kenya and Djibouti-Ethiopia, as well as the major breakthrough at the BRI conference in Beijing last May. He used remarks by the Chinese Ambassador to the Republic of South Africa, Lin Songtian, to draw out the contrast between the British outlook and that of China. Ambassador Lin wrote, in his response to former U.S. Secretary of State Rex Tillerson's attacks on Chinese involvement in Africa, "What they really want is to keep Africa as it was, poor and divided, to be always controlled by others. What they worry about is Africa's realization of economic independence with China's support. What they worry about is a strong Africa that can no longer be ordered around politically."

After a review of the decades of work by the LaRouche movement for world development, including the World Land-Bridge proposal of 1997, Ross reported the recent, exciting progress in Africa—focusing on the

Ross briefly reviewed other African development requirements and projects—transportation, water (including the Transaqua plan to refill Lake Chad), and especially energy—and concluded by contrasting the economic record and approach of Lyndon LaRouche to the overwhelming majority of economists, who demonstrated their abject professional failure by failing, in 2007, to see the crisis right in front of their noses.

LaRouche's success is based on his unique economic breakthroughs, made in the tradition of the American System of Alexander Hamilton, which sees scientific progress

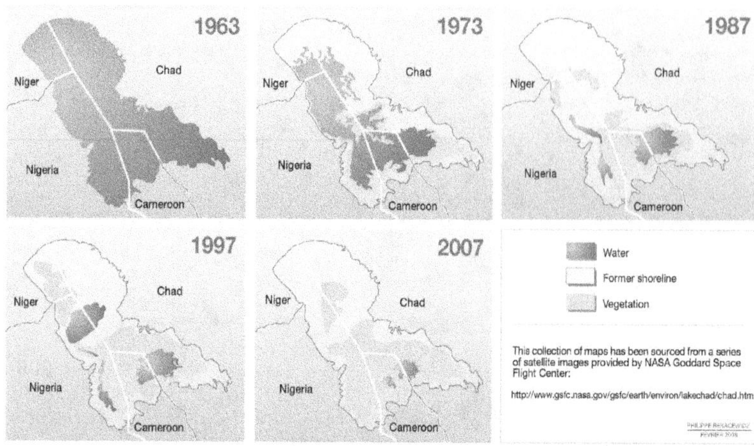


*Shrinkage of water volume in Lake Chad: 1963-2000.*

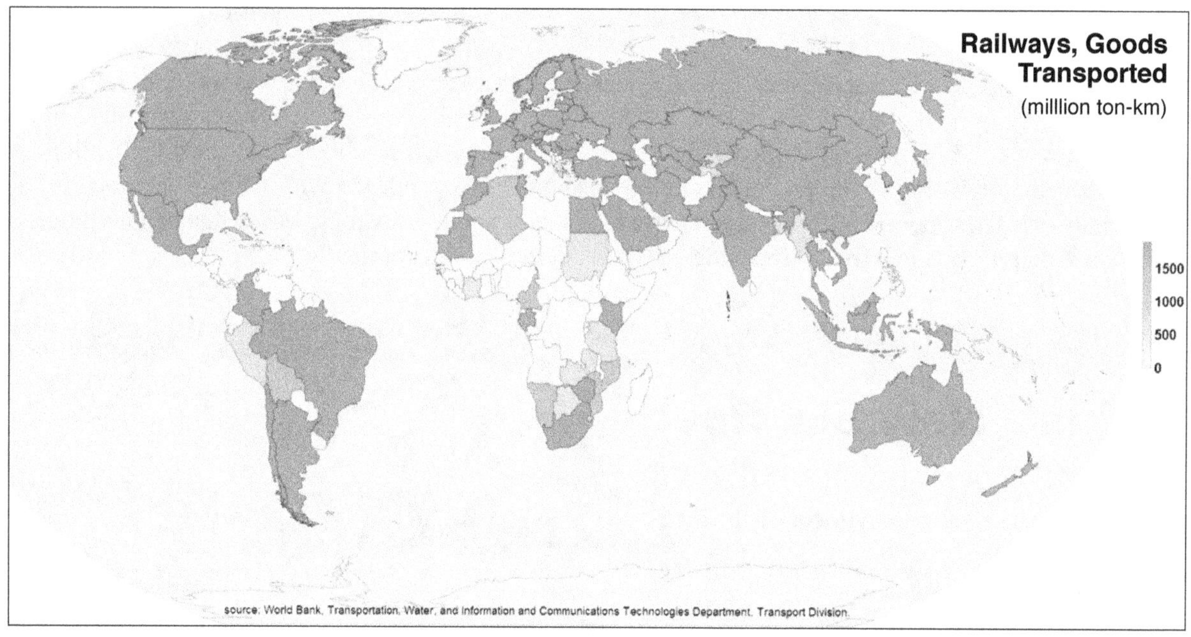


developing the productive powers of labor as the absolute basis of economic growth. From this economic outlook, LaRouche's "Four Laws" are the needed policy for the United States today. By our nation acting on this basis, we will have the ability to finally eliminate the British Empire from the face of the earth. In doing so, we will have achieved a world-historic objective of unique importance, and which the United States itself is in a unique position to achieve. This is our mission today.

*Mombasa-Nairobi Standard Gauge Railway.*

ThinkGeoEnergy

DR. XU WENHONG

# Join the One Belt, One Road Initiative

*Dr. Xu Wenhong has a PhD in Law, and is the Associate Researcher and Deputy Secretary General of the Center for Belt and Road Studies at the Chinese Academy of Social Sciences. This is a transcript of his statement at the Schiller Institute conference, "Dona Nobis Pacem— Grant Us Peace, Through Economic Development," convened in New York City on Saturday, June 9, 2018.*

Schiller Institute

*Dr. Xu Wenhong, Deputy Secretary General, Center for Belt & Road Studies, Chinese Academy of Social Sciences.*

Dear Mme. Helga Zepp-LaRouche, Dear participants of this event:

Ladies and Gentlemen, good morning. I'm very honored to be here to speak on One Belt, One Road topic. In 2007, when I met for the first time with Mme. Helga LaRouche, I got to know from her, that she and her Schiller Institute have been promoting the Third Land-Bridge Project for many years. She and the Schiller Institute still are one of the pioneers in this field. On top of that, you have so many achievements: Congratulations!

Actually, the One Belt, One Road Initiative is an up-dated version of the Third Land-Bridge Project. "One Belt" means the Silk Road Economic Belt. It was coined by Chinese President Xi Jinping in his speech on Sept. 27, 2013, at Nazarbayev University in Kazakhstan. "One Road" means the 21st Century Maritime Silk Road, which was first mentioned by the Chinese President Xi Jinping in his speech, addressing the National Assembly in Malaysia on Oct. 7, 2013. From that, we call these two terms, in short, "One Belt, One Road."

Western people compare the One Belt, One Road Initiative to the Marshall Plan, but the Initiative is totally different from the Marshall Plan. It's much more meaningful, it's much bigger than the Marshall Plan.

The One Belt, One Road Initiative has three principles: consensus, win-win, and sharing. That means, although the framework of the One Belt, One Road Initiative should be based on well-recognized consensus,

only with consensus could more be achieved. And all parties should have equal rights within the Initiative, and all parties could equally benefit from this Initiative.

The One Belt, One Road Initiative focussed on five factors, which are: policy coordination, transportation connectivity, unimpeded trade, finance cooperation, and the people-to-people exchange. When we're talking about the policy coordination, we should at least be talking about four levels of coordination. That means we should be based on the common understanding of surroundings; common understanding of coming tasks; when we're talking about transportation connectivity, we are talking about seaports, airports, gas pipelines, cable pipeline, and other infrastructure constructions. When we're talking about unimpeded trade, we know that for many years, China has become the top trading partner to many countries. When we talk about financial cooperation, we know that within the framework of One Belt, One Road Initiative, we have built the Asian Infrastructure Investment Bank, the Silk Road Fund, and other financial institutions. When we talk about people-to-people exchange, we know that at this time, in 2017 alone, we have had more than 100 meetings, with Chinese people going abroad for travel. At the same time, there are more and more tourists from all over the world coming to China.

Also, when we're talking about the aims and goals of the One Belt, One Road Initiative we know that we are fighting for three communities: The community of common interest, the community of common responsibilities, and the community of shared destinies. These communities are not military alliances, but new forms for economic cooperation.

To sum up, with this Initiative, China is ready to join hands with all willing countries, to fight for a just, fair, reasonable world order, to make a better world, to make the global village full of peace and stability, to make the whole global village full of peace and prosperity.

I hope you all can understand the true meaning of One Belt, One Road Initiative, and join this initiative.

Thank you.

DMITRY POLYANSKIY

# Our Eurasian Economic Integration Concept Harmonizes with the BRI

*Dmitry Polyanskiy is the First Deputy Permanent Representative of the Russian Federation to the United Nations. These are his remarks to the Schiller Institute conference, "Dona Nobis Pacem— Grant Us Peace, Through Economic Development," convened in New York City on Saturday, June 9, 2018. He spoke on Panel 1 of the conference: "A New Paradigm of Global Relations, Ending Geopolitics—The Four Powers."*

*Dmitry Polyanskiy*

nation almost disappeared, Russia and its leader, Alexander II, allied with our nation and were instrumental in preserving it. That is, together with Abraham Lincoln, Alexander II freed serfs in Russia and slaves in America.

In the 20th century, at a very dark time in European history, when Russia had been invaded by Hitler's armies, and even prior to that time, President Franklin Roosevelt made sure that the United States joined with the Soviet Union and fought together against fascism. That was a proud moment.

**Dennis Speed:** In introducing the next speaker, I want to point something out. At a very dark time in American history, between 1861 and 1865, when our

Today, it is the intent, certainly of the Schiller Institute, and as we understand it, apparently of the President of the United States, to make sure that there is a new form of cooperation, of peace through development. It is our hope that, today, as you listen to the next speaker, you think of ways in which you can contribute to making sure that a New Paradigm of global relations that ends geopolitics, actually comes into being.

It is my honor to introduce to you Dmitry Polyanskiy, First Deputy Permanent Representative of the Russian Federation to the United Nations. [applause]

**Dmitry Polyanskiy:** Thank you very much, thank you. I'm very much honored to be here. To be quite frank, I didn't prepare a special speech for this event, but I'm absolutely open to any suggestions, any comments, and I would be most ready to answer your questions.

The topic of your discussion I think is very important: "Grant us peace through economic development." This is very much echoing the policy of the Russian government, because we are open to fruitful and mutually beneficial cooperation, with all the countries in the world, without any exception. Some people may assume that there is a certain anti-American mood in my country, because of all the obstacles that we're facing in the world arena, because of all this public criticism that we're hearing. But this is not true!

Russia still remains very friendly towards the United States; we still maintain a very big interest in what's happening in your country. We know that your country has a great history; we know that Americans are very wise people, and they will make good decisions. If I'm not mistaken, Winston Churchill once said that Americans always make the right decisions, but only after they have tried all the wrong ones! [laughter]

So I think eventually the good will prevail. Maybe we're very close to it. It very much depends on our interaction with Washington. It's not because we are big states, it's because we are responsible states. We understand very well what's happening in the world; we understand the challenges, we understand the possibilities, and I'm absolutely sure that our interlocutors also understand how the world can benefit from close cooperation and trust between Russia and the United States.

I think trust is the key word here. In the United Nations we are working as hard as we can, for the re-estab-

lishment of trust. We discuss all the topics with our partners, including American partners. We don't have any taboos in our discussion, and we value very much the cooperation that we have.

## We Will Welcome a Settlement with North Korea

Speaking about trust, I would say that during the last several years, maybe ten years, maybe a little bit less, we have advanced very much on the path of the establishment of trust and mutually beneficial cooperation with China. China is Russia's most important partner. We very much like the Chinese people. We expanded to a large extent the exchanges between our peoples—people-to-people contact. There are a lot of Russian tourists in China right now, and there are lot of Chinese tourists in Moscow. The Chinese language is now very widely taught in Russia, including in schools; the Russian language is very popular in China, as well.

So we are making steps towards better understanding each other. It's not always easy to read the Chinese mind for us, really. It's a big challenge. But we do not teach others how to live and what to do and what not to do. We're not intrusive; we're not assertive. And that's why we proceed from a mutual understanding of respect, for history, for traditions. We really believe that being different doesn't mean being dangerous, and that is the cornerstone of our relations with other countries, including China.

Our "Pivot to the East," which was declared several years ago, is not something that is being done in retaliation to the attitude of the West. This was a long-awaited move that we should have really taken, regardless of any elements of our relations with the United States and with the West. So, we really should have made this step a long time ago, and the events that followed, after the crisis in relations between Russia and the West, after the heaps and oodles of misunderstandings that we have now in our relations, these events, of course, accelerated our mutual movement towards each other with China.

So we have very actively supported the One Belt, One Road initiative. We have a lot of common projects together. We have an understanding that the concept of Eurasian integration that is being promoted by Russia and by some of our partners from CIS countries, does not contradict, but even, I would say, supplements very well the initiative of One Belt, One Road.

We include these topics in all the consultations that we have with Beijing. Recently, we signed an agreement on cooperation between the Eurasian Economic Union and China. This is not a free trade agreement. A free trade agreement is a very challenging move: Maybe it will be the next step. But this cooperation agreement is something that will really bring us closer together. It gives us additional leverage and tools to promote cooperation: first of all, economic cooperation; streamlining procedures to avoid red tape; and again, bringing our peoples and our countries towards each other.

It's very important to point out that Russia and China are not making friends against somebody. It's not a closed club. It's not something that we are together like, you know, a G2 [laughter], forming some alliance against America, against the West; no, absolutely not. We understand that our Chinese friends and partners have very important economic interests in the United States, in Europe, and it would be crazy of us to demand that China abolish these policies and absolutely be friends only with us. It would be a bit childish and I would say unreasonable to be such jealous people about cooperation of other countries.

So, we support every move in the world that leads to some kind of detente, that leads to some kind of better understanding among different countries. We supported the move by President Trump to engage in negotiations with North Korea. Some people said that Russia was jealous because Russia is not participating. It's OK with us. If you guys can come to terms with North Korea, we will welcome it, really, very sincerely. If you want us to participate at some later stage, we will participate. If you don't want us to participate, we don't want to participate. No problem. We don't want to bother you.

## Let's Work Together!

We want peace and cooperation to prevail, bilaterally, multilaterally, in any format possible. We are against hate speech, and we are against neglecting the principle of presumption of innocence, which is very often omitted vis-à-vis Russia today, unfortunately, in many cases. We have to face this on a daily basis.

We really hope that there will be better understanding between us and the people in Washington. There was a very difficult time, until recently. Today, there are, I would say, some glimpses of hope. Right now, relations between Russia and the United States are very, very fragile, and I would say that we need to work a little bit, and to understand whether such relations are sustainable, or if it's just a matter of chance. But we have hope. We are a patient people.

Thanks to economic sanctions, Russia has become almost self-sustaining in many spheres, first of all with regard to the European Union. Five, six years ago, things were different, but now Russia is producing such a large number of agricultural products, like cheese, for example. I was absolutely sure that we were incapable of making good cheese [laughter]. But, I turned out to be absolutely wrong. If you come to the Russian shops right now, you will see there are really very good, and very high-quality cheeses, beers, I don't know—everything else. So we are not depending on the West any more in this regard.

There are, however, certain things for which we really are still dependent, such as pharmaceuticals and medicines, so we are not really keen to disrupt cooperation, but we will cope. Even if the time comes when it will be harder and more difficult for us, Russia will cope. Russia will survive. No problem.

But we really hope that people here will become more mature in terms of international politics, that they will feel more responsibility for what they are doing, and we will be able to join our efforts, in wider formats. I heard recently that there are ideas of bringing Russia into the G8, for example, but this is not very real for us at this stage. Actually, we initially preferred the G20 to the G8, and I think that this format is better now. It's a more or less balanced economic format, which better reflects the situation in today's world. So we would be very keen to promote that format instead.

That's it in a nutshell. I don't know whether my remarks were helpful or not, but I can assure you that we would not spare any effort to bring our countries together and to make our world a safer place.

So I will sit down. If you have any questions on any topic not raised here, I would be glad to answer them. Thank you very much. [applause]

# A New Paradigm of Global Relations, Ending Geopolitics—The Four Powers

*The following is an edited transcript of the Panel 1 Question and Answer session at the Schiller Institute conference, "Dona Nobis Pacem—Grant Us Peace, Through Economic Development," convened in New York City on Saturday, June 9, 2018.*

**Dennis Speed:** We're now open for discussion and questions.

**Elliot Greenspan:** As Helga emphasized in her remarks, you've got the Shanghai Cooperation Organization (SCO) event ongoing this weekend; you've got the North Korea-U.S. summit in three days; then there's the discussion of the possibility of a U.S.-Russia summit perhaps as early as July, and so on. I would like to ask Helga and the representative of Russia, both, if you look forward over the next period, what your thoughts are about the prospects, the kind of discussion coming out of this weekend, the kind of discussion which could be taken up between President Trump and President Putin, the subject areas, the potential to transform the very significant prospects which are ongoing, but to build on that?

## Possibilities for Transformation

**Dmitry Polyanskiy:** I wouldn't overestimate the importance of the top political level. Of course, it's important if two leaders come together and establish terms on certain issues, but I would think more important is the dialogue among ordinary people, among civil society. The problem I see—I'm here in America only four months—is I see that a lot of people really don't understand what's happening in Russia, and have very clear anti-Russian sentiments that are being driven by some pieces of information that I really don't understand. Like everybody's asking me questions in the street, when they know that I'm Russian,—very simple people ask me, "Why did you meddle in our elections?" I say, "How do you know?" They say, "They say that you're meddling." "OK, I will say that I'm from the Moon—will you believe me?" That's the level of expertise, really! [laughter]

It's more important to rebuild trust between our two peoples. In the beginning of the 1990s, we Russians were initially very much welcoming the American presence in our country. We were really hoping that Americans would bring us economic expertise, good advice, money, and the world would be prosperous and there would be no more conflicts.

We were a bit naive. Since then, we've lost a lot of trust in your country, frankly speaking. We feel that there is a very clear hidden agenda behind almost everything you are doing. And even if our Presidents come together, even if there is some kind of détente and—I don't know—love, between our countries, I think that we shouldn't be too optimistic.

We need to re-establish the trust and reestablish the desire of the common people to see each other in a positive light and to do away with all these stereotypes that we have. We need more Russians to come to America, and more Americans to come to Russia, to bring our people together, to bring young people together, to understand that we are really not enemies but friends, and we can do a lot together.

So I would accent ordinary people meeting ordinary people, rather than some artificial summits and benchmarks—they come and go, but our countries remain. My countrymen are very friendly, very optimistic, we don't bear a grudge against the United States. There's a personal grudge against some politicians. We understand that you're a big country and we really need to have some time to understand what's happening and how to deal with it. We are a patient people; we're not pressing you.

Thank you. [applause]

Jason Ross, co-author of "Extending the New Silk Road to West Asia and Africa: a Vision of an Economic Renaissance," speaking at the Schiller Institute conference.



## The Role of Leadership in World History

**Helga Zepp-LaRouche:** I obviously believe in the value of peoples-to-peoples communication, getting to know each other's culture, the beauty of each other's culture. Normally you find that ordinary people are warm-hearted. Most people, simple people, tend to be much better than the official institutions—at least in the West I can say that.

However, I think we are in a historical period which is *really* dramatically changing. In my view, we are experiencing the collapse of an era. I have several times made the point that the kind of change we are experiencing right now is as big, if not bigger, than the change from the Middle Ages to modern times. If you look at the axioms characteristic for the Middle Ages, in Europe, you had scholasticism, you had the Peripatetics, the neo-Aristotelians, you had witch-belief. And then came the Italian Renaissance and because of the work of Nicholas of Cusa—Nikolaus Cusansky—and the re-introduction of Plato, who was brought by the Orthodox delegation coming to the Council of Florence, you had a Renaissance of Platonism. All of sudden, you had a completely new image of man, a modern image of the individual, and the role of the state as being responsible for the common good, which did not exist before, and out of that developed modern science and Classical art as we know it.

That was a paradigm shift. We are experiencing right now a similar paradigm shift. In the past you had empires, you had colonialism. The consequences of colonialism are with us, still, to the present day. Africa still in large part suffers from that. It's the same in many other developing countries—the result of hundreds of years of colonialism, and for that matter, the IMF conditionalities, which did not allow for any development.

But then came the New Silk Road idea of Xi Jinping. The reason why it's so extremely attractive and gaining so much support, is because it addresses exactly the fundamental needs of Africa and Latin America, and even parts of Europe. What you see right now, in my view, is the emergence of New Paradigm about man, about how nations can work together, a new model of great-power relationships, which is being implemented right now in a perfect way between Russia and China, and which Xi Jinping has also offered to the United States. There is a much bigger emphasis on innovation, on the excellence of education. We are witnessing right now a transformation to what I would call the Adulthood of Mankind.

If we can overcome the remaining big problems which *are* big—for example, the West is still threatened with a danger of a financial collapse; the Deutsche Bank situation; the Italian banking system is not the only one which is bankrupt, many banks are actually bankrupt.

Even discounting the derivatives, the situation is one of a total lack of liquidity. So that is a big challenge, because if you have an uncontrolled collapse of the financial system, everything will be thrown into chaos.

**Transformation Will Not Be Easy**

I'm not saying that the present transformation is going to be easy, but I think that in addition to civil society exchanges, you do need leadership from the top. We have the very good fortune of having outstanding leaders right now. President Xi Jinping is an absolutely outstanding personality, deeply Confucian, educated; President Putin is also an absolutely incredible strategist who continues to outwit those evil forces that have worked to reduce Russia's status after the collapse of the Soviet Union, to that of a third world, raw-materials producer. President Putin has been able to reverse that, not totally yet, but he's on an absolutely remarkable path of doing that. Hopefully we will have some new important leaders emerging. Leadership in these times is very important.

We proposed, very early on, a summit between Trump and Putin. The entire Russiagate operation was designed—by piling it on that he was in the White House only because of Putin, and Russian meddling—to prevent Trump from fulfilling his election promise to improve the relationship between the United States with Russia. This was all designed to box him in. He wasn't able to meet Putin until the G20 in Hamburg last year; and was forced to meet Putin only on the sidelines of some other summit. But having an in-depth discussion, Putin and Trump being able to define new conceptions for the world, is very important, in my view.

There are many conceptions which need to be discussed. For example, the Belt and Road Initiative being integrated with the Eurasian Economic Union, gives the concept for a Eurasian integration from Vladivostok to Lisbon. I think this is something which should be placed on the agenda. We have campaigned to get the United States on board with a Four Power Agreement, so it's not a contradiction to a Eurasian conception.

A new international security architecture, based on such economic cooperation, is very urgent. There is, as both leaders have said many times, the danger of a new arms race, which is really a terrible waste and also very dangerous. So the question of a new international security architecture would be also such a subject.

I think it's very important to do both. People need to meet and know other people, to love the other culture, to know it. But I think leadership is also urgently required in a historical moment like this. [applause]

**How Does the New Paradigm Differ
From the Old?**

**Question:** I hope that Schiller Institute can translate the conference Invitation into Chinese, because it's a new area for me. I'm a linguist and teach Chinese at Howard University.

My question to Helga is, what's a "New Paradigm"? Can you identify it and explain what the difference is between the New Paradigm and the old paradigm?

And for Dmitry, my question is, what's the strategic partnership of Russia and the Eurasian Economic Union, and difference with the G8? And, can you identify and explain the difference? Thank you.

**Zepp-LaRouche:** The old paradigm is what I would associate with the present, dominant axiomatic belief-structure of the West, which unfortunately is characterized by geopolitics, the idea that Europe must unite to be able to play their role against other great powers, such as China, Russia, and now, with Trump as President, even against the United States—especially against the United States. The old paradigm is also neo-liberalism in economics; it's the idea of a neo-liberal moral value system. It's an image of man which is associated with the idea that man is either only a more advanced animal—which you hear a lot—or that there is no way to establish a knowable truth, that every opinion is equally good. In the cultural realm, the old paradigm really has become the idea that "everything goes": There is no perversity, no violence, no ugliness which is not allowed. Everyone, according to the old paradigm, can insist on their personal right to be pornographic, to be violent: If it's what want someone wants, it is okay.

All of this is symptomatic of an absolutely decaying culture, of a system in its death agony. For example, a year and a half ago, Russian Foreign Minister Lavrov gave a press conference in which he said the values that the West are trying to export to our country are no longer the values which were passed down from generation to generation, but these are what he called "post-Christian values," exactly the idea that "everything goes." That's really the problem: You have a system in which it's the survival of the fittest. It's an inhuman image of man. The fact that we have this drug epidemic in the United States, that we have an increasing suicide rate, that we have such violence in the schools: These are all symptoms of this old paradigm.

I absolutely contrast that with the New Paradigm, which defines humanity from the standpoint of the future. How do we want mankind to be in a hundred years from now, or even in a thousand years from now? Do we still want to have wars? Or, don't you think that the kind of international cooperation which we see right now in space cooperation should be the model for how we organize relations among people on the planet Earth?

## Look to the Paradigm of Space Cooperation

German astronaut Alexander Gerst just went up to the International Space Station together with an American female astronaut and a Russian cosmonaut. When you listen to these astronauts you get a feeling—their collaboration, working on exploration, their efforts to better understand the universe. There are two trillion galaxies out there! Can you imagine two *trillion* galaxies? And what do we know about them? Absolutely little. Everything we explore in space very much leads us to realize that we are the only species known so far—for sure the only species on Earth—that can travel into space. Why? Because we are the only creative species.

The New Paradigm is basically the idea that, that which combines individuals and nations is our common identity as creative beings, and the future kind of healthy cooperation to be expected among people. I have the image of every child having access to universal education, having no material need. Not having excessive riches, but enough so that every child can study universal history, every child can study other languages and other cultures, can have a science education and a Classical art education. That people will have quite different wishes and aspirations.

If you talk to excellent scientists, they never are greedy, they never want to accumulate enormous stock portfolios; they want to do their science. If you talk to good artists, do they want to become millionaires? No! They want to be excellent and truth-seeking in their art, and that's what gives them a fulfilling life.

So the New Paradigm is human beings become really human by developing their creativity and relating to each other on the basis of the other person's creativity, creating something good for all of mankind out of it. [applause]

## The Role of Eurasia

**Polyanskiy:** I will try to be short in answering your question because it's very easy: We shouldn't compare the G8 with the Eurasian Economic Union, because these two are absolutely different. The G8 is a kind of discussion club: It's a forum of eight—now seven—heads of state plus some ministers that come together. They don't have a charter. They don't have any treaties among them. It's just a temporary construction.

We value the G20 very much because it comprises other states which are very important, like China, like India, like Indonesia, like Russia, so it would be very difficult to formulate any economic agenda in the world without the participation of these states. I think everybody understands this.

As for the Eurasian Economic Union, it's the organization of economic integration. We have a treaty; we ceded parts of national sovereignty at this supranational level. So it can be compared, more or less, with the European Union. You have the Eurasian Economic Commission, which has certain prerogatives to work in certain spheres on behalf of our five states. And we are trying to enlarge this supranational responsibility.

So this is our response to the trend of globalization. We believe in integration, we believe in interaction between different countries and peoples, and our response to it was the Eurasian economic project and the Eurasian Economic Union. So, it is an open project which promotes the idea of integration of integrations, to bring to one table, the European Union; so it's kind of an expansionist and integrationist project; and the G8 is like a closed club—I don't know, something like that.

**Diane Sare:** I'm Diane Sare, one of the directors of the Schiller Institute Chorus. I want to say a couple of things. First, on the perception of the American public, when you have people such as [former Director of the CIA] John Brennan, who testified before Congress saying, "I don't do evidence," who then becomes an anchor person at NBC [laughter], that does call into question the legitimacy of what's in the U.S. news media.

## Music and Putin's Visit to Austria

I want to ask you some questions about Putin's visit to Austria. It appears he was very warmly received. I was particularly happy about his short meeting with the very young musician and composer Alma Deutscher. I also understand there were street festivals celebrating the musical culture of Austria and Russia. You may be able to confirm if they declared 2018 to be the Year of Music, something that I heard, which is very optimistic.

As you may know, a year and a half ago, on our

Schiller Institute/Susan Kokinda

*Dimitry Polyanskiy, Russia's First Deputy Representative to the United Nations, speaking at the Schiller Institute conference.*

Christmas Day, we received the horrible news of the plane crash carrying the Alexandrov Ensemble. For many of us, particularly those of us involved in music, it was like a punch in the stomach; it was a horrible loss. Last year and this year, we organized a memorial at the Tear-Drop Monument in New Jersey. Many Americans actually are very concerned that there be peaceful relations between our countries, and also have more knowledge [of each other]. It turned out that the father or uncle of the chaplain who spoke at that memorial service had been the translator at the famous meeting at the Elbe in World War II.

But I thought you might have something to say about this question of music—if it is the Year of Music. Also, I wanted to personally extend to you—and I don't wish to impose—but anyone you wish to send, we will give you tickets to our concert tomorrow at 4:00 o'clock. I'd love to see you or any representatives there. We'll give you good seats. [laughter]

**Polyanskiy:** Thank you very much for these kind words and I'm really very grateful to you and your colleagues for what you're doing in the memory of the Alexandrov Choir. I can tell you that the choir, of course in a different composition, has now reemerged. There will be a number of concerts of this new choir in the coming days in Moscow and St. Petersburg. We hope it will become as popular and as famous as the previous

crew who, unfortunately, lost their lives.

## Music and Culture Are Universal

Answering your question: Music and culture are universal values. They don't need translation, everybody understands them. We have a lot of students in Moscow in specialized institutions—the Conservatorium and academies of music and fine arts—and they don't need interpreters, they don't need translators, they understand very well what people want to say. Of course this is a universal tool, it will remain so regardless of the political conjuncture, regardless of all the problems we may face, because we will still listen to the music, and people will still ask themselves the questions, "What was the country, what was the situation, that really helped this piece of music to be born?" And if it's attributed to Russia, of course, people will understand that Russia is not some country that you really can sideline somewhere on the sidewalk and ignore.

## The Rich Classical Music Culture of Moscow

We have an enormous potential, an enormous cultural life. I really miss a lot Moscow culture life here. The cultural life is very rich here in New York, of course; it's one of the centers of cultural life. But still, in Moscow, cultural life is a bit different. We placed a greater emphasis on theaters, on music; we have several platforms for Classical music, and I'm really looking forward to going back on my vacation and seeing my friends there. I have a lot of friends among artists, among performers. I encourage very much the cultural exchanges with any country—with the United States, with Europe.

This brings me to your other question, Putin's visit to Austria. Austria is a very particular country. First of all, the Austrians are very stubborn. They really are neutral and it's difficult to prove to them your point of view, if you don't have enough reason. That was always so. I served in Austria for several months in our bilateral embassy, so I like that country very much. They are very grateful to Russia, to Soviet Union. They still remember that Soviet Union liberated them from Nazism. We actually are one of the guarantors of the Austrian republic, which is a legal status. And sometimes we act as guarantors, still now. There are four states involved—this is a post World War II construction, so we play a certain role in Austrian politics.

That's why it's not very easy to bring into Austrian minds the idea that Russia should be ostracized and isolated and ignored—they resist this idea, traditionally. That's why we maintained dialogue with this country for many, many years, and nothing serious has changed, even in the context of the sanctions and all these problems that we are having with many countries of the world. Many of them are partners with Austria, but that doesn't change very much.

That's why it's very symbolic that our President visited Austria after his reelection right now. This is a gesture to the people there who came to power and who are very friendly, who are very eager to cooperate. It's not that we are trying to use them to create certain instability in Europe, to break the ranks among the European Union. It's up to them to decide what they are doing; but there are more and more voices saying that the sanctions against Russia are detrimental to the European Union.

It's not a very big problem for the United States, because our two countries' economic cooperation is very symbolic on many issues. But when it comes to Europe, people really are losing a lot because of the sanctions: They have lost work places, they have lost contracts. Imagine how difficult it will be now for producers of agricultural products to try to reenter the Russian market, when we've gotten used to our own production. Why do we need something that's more expensive, when the quality is the same and the price is much less? So they have already lost this market. Car producers also have difficulties. Those who took political decisions to leave Russia, regret it now. But well, politics comes above economics here, and this is not right.

The Austrians managed to keep a balance and always remain a bridge between Russia and the European Union. Since Soviet times, as you may know, Austria was the first sort of hub for Soviet gas coming into Europe, and this is also very symbolic.

## Cultural Exchange and the Role of Austria

That's why it's not a coincidence. We have programs of cultural exchanges and years of culture, not only with Austria but with many countries. Even with such countries as United Kingdom, regardless of how difficult our political relations might be, people still want to listen to Russian music, to see Russian ballet, and to visit Russia. There are a lot of English fans who are coming to visit World Cup these days, although there were different terrible stories about Russians beating English fans, bears walking in the streets, and I don't know [laughter]. All this is coming back.

I think people here and people in Europe are much wiser sometimes than politicians; they know what they want, and it's very difficult to spoil with this political, I would say, foam which is on the top, to spoil the deep-rooted feelings and mutual interests between them, between Russians and Europeans, and Americans. And I hope this will prevail in the nearest future.

**Question:** My question is for you, Mr. Polyanskiy. The Schiller Institute and the LaRouche movement more generally have been involved for decades in trying to communicate to the Americans the role of the British in determining U.S. policy as well as U.S. public opinion. A few months ago, Maria Zakharova outlined some of the really horrific history of the British Empire. And now, with the ongoing attacks against our elected President, we are beginning to see evidence surfacing of the role of British intelligence in trying to undermine the decision of the American voters in electing President Trump.

My question is whether you think among the Russian people or among the Russian institutions, there is an understanding of the distinction between the United States and the British poisoning of U.S. policy and public opinion?

**Polyanskiy:** That's a very philosophic question, I would say. I didn't analyze this as deeply as you, the role of British intelligence and Britain in influencing public opinion. I know that United Kingdom and United States are very close—you speak one language, more or less, so you really have the same values, and you have no constraints in travelling. That's why it's understandable that there is a mutual, I would say, influence, between London and Washington, and this is very good.

As for the intelligence, well, United Kingdom is not the only country that possesses intelligence in the world. There are other countries, which can have counterintelligence, and this is the rule of the game. Every action causes certain reaction to this action, so the stronger they try to do something bad, the stronger will be the response, everywhere, and I'm absolutely sure that in this country, people will understand that they are being manipulated at some point, and they will make their conclusions themselves. We're not imposing our opinion anywhere. But we like the things about James Bond, really. [laughter] Let's keep the image of efficient British intelligence based on these films, OK? [applause]

### Youth and an Alliance Against War

**Question:** My question is very simple, for Mr. Polyanskiy: What do you think of the idea of young people advocating for the alliance *against* war?

**Polyanskiy:** That's a good instinct, but why only young people? I think everybody wants to live. I think young people maybe don't have a lot of institutional memory about what has happened in previous years, and this is an asset. They do not prejudge the situation, from the stereotypes that sometimes we have and our elder colleagues do have.

Youth is the key to everything. We do everything for our children, for our grandchildren. And of course, their interests should prevail, and they shouldn't be ignored. Take this country, the demographic situation is one way; in Russia, it is another, but close to that of this country. But if you take Africa, for example, you will see that the number of very young people, for example ages 14, 15, are close to 50% or even more, which is a big, big challenge, and it's a question of education that should be really put on the agenda. Because, well, it's our responsibility, it's the key to everything—education and good atmosphere, good environment.

It's our task to give the conditions and basis for these young people to get the understanding of life, to get ideals that would not be harmful to the world, that would promote cooperation and friendship, that would exclude hate speech—not to zombie them, but to give them an open mind. If there are more and more open-minded people, not biased, not limited by any ideological framework, that would be beneficial to all of us. Thank you.

**Speed:** We're at the conclusion of our first session, and I wonder, Helga, if you want to respond to either of the last exchanges, or just want to give a summary statement at this point?

**Zepp-LaRouche:** I think that the historical moment is totally exciting. There are periods where things are sort of stable, normal, decades go by when nothing much changes, and nothing much can be done, because history is in a calmer mode.

### A Moment of Epochal Change

This is clearly not the case of our present time. We are today seeing changes that are so dramatic. Almost every day you have some breaking development, where, as I said in my presentation, new strategic alignments are occurring, new conceptions are being put forward. And I think it's a very exciting moment to be alive. You cannot always change certain objective conditions because they're too big or too gigantic to be influenced, but a time of such epochal transformation is also the best time when ideas can matter.

I can only say that the ideas of my husband Lyndon LaRouche, who has been working on these kinds of conceptions of a just new world economic order for more than half a century (as a matter of fact, probably more like 75 years, or even longer than that) but now these conceptions are influential—what Jason Ross discussed in his presentation—LaRouche's work in terms of having this idea that the underdevelopment of the developing sector must be overcome; the many, many scientific conceptions he revived, in terms of the 2,500 years of European civilization. A lot of these things are now coming into being, because some powerful countries are working in this direction and realizing them.

So, the power of ideas is absolutely crucial, and we are very fortunate. I'm not diminishing the dangers which are still there. The possibility of a big war is not by far eliminated. But I want everyone to have an optimistic sense that we can experience in the very near future, in our lifetimes, a completely different world, *if* we activate ourselves now and fight for that better future. Because right now, we have a constellation of many countries in the world acting optimistically. The mood in African countries is absolutely changed; Latin America is changed; and also in Eurasia, many countries and peoples in those countries are talking about the future in a much more optimistic way than we see it for the most part in the United States or in Germany for that matter.

If people have a vision, that with their own work, they can help to create a more human world, and they believe that change is absolutely possible, I think we can do it, and we should be happy about it, and be self-assured and confident in our ability to make a better world. [applause]



Now Only LaRouche's Methods Will Work   

## Choosing Creativity—Not Tragedy—
## In Economics and Statecraft

DENNIS SPEED

# The LaRouche Method:
# Seed-Crystal of a New Culture

*Dennis Speed is the U.S. Northeast Coordinator of the Schiller Institute. This is his address to the Schiller Institute conference, "Dona Nobis Pacem—Grant Us Peace, Through Economic Development," convened in New York City on Saturday, June 9, 2018.*

**Dennis Speed:** We chose to call this panel "Choosing Creativity—Not Tragedy—In Economics and Statecraft." We are going to try to place Cicero, who is not here with us—Lyndon La-Rouche—in the room, rather than the various Brutuses and Cassiuses and Julius Caesars and others that might occupy, or seem to occupy, the tragedy of today's landscape.

President Donald Trump does not intend to be a tragic figure, but many Americans intend him to be that. The American people, unfortunately, don't really exactly understand the concept of tragedy.

One thing about Lyndon LaRouche, and our association—those of us privileged enough to be with him for so many years—is that Lyn and his association always had a really good time. We had a lot of fun, and have a lot of fun. And the way we do that is by destroying axioms.

Lyndon LaRouche rediscovered the American Presidency, particularly in the aftermath of the assassinations of JFK, RFK, and Martin Luther King. Of course, his collaboration with Ronald Reagan is a very impor-

Schiller Institute

*Dennis Speed*

tant element of that rediscovery of the American Presidency. He demonstrated to all of us, to the world, as he put it, "I only have to convince one guy -and that's the President of the United States." And that's what he did in the 1980s, around what was called the Strategic Defense Initiative.

He wasn't very loved very much for that: He spent five years in prison as a result of that successful, very happy, and very (in one sense) humorous assault on the institutions of the oligarchy.

### The Significance of Dr. King Today

We're going to go right now to Lyn, and let Lyn speak directly to you, as Presidents speak. He spoke in January of 2004, at the very point that something would come slouching toward Bethlehem out of Chicago, called Barack Obama. Speaking in Talladega, Alabama, on the occasion of the Martin Luther King celebration, here's what he had to say:

**Lyndon LaRouche:** We're in trouble.... Look at the world. The world faces a great crisis. And he United States faces a great crisis, in dealing with the world. The largest concentrations of population of the world are in China, for example, at one point, 1.3 billion or more; India over 1 billion; then you have Pakistan, Bangladesh, and the countries of Southeast Asia: This

*Dr. Martin Luther King, Jr.*

public domain

is the greatest concentration of population on this planet. It's an emerging part of the world. The question is, what's the relationship of the United States to these people of Asia, who represent, by and large, different cultural backgrounds, than those of us in the United States or in Western Europe?

How are we going to find peace in a troubled world? How are we going to find reconciliation in a troubled world, with countries which have turned against us, because of the war policies of [Vice President Dick] Cheney and some others?

So, we face the situation.

Now, go back a little bit, to the time that Bill Clinton was inaugurated as President. Now, think about something some of you know about: Think about the status of the Black Caucus, Legislative Caucus, or Black Congressional Caucus, in 1993, when Bill Clinton came into the White House. Now—go through the list of names: Where are those people, and their replacements today? There has been a winnowing out of the political achievements, throughout the country, of the black caucuses.

This is the problem I deal with constantly, actually from 1996 on. It became worse, accelerated, brutally.

So, we do not face a new problem today, in one sense. We face the same problem, in principle, that Martin faced, and faced successfully. And I would propose, that in the lesson of

Martin Luther King, and his life, there is something we can learn today, which brings him back to life, as if he were standing here, alive, today. There's something special about his life, his development, which should be captured today, by us, not only in addressing the problems of our nation, which are becoming terrible; but the problems of our relationship with the world as a whole. How are we going to deal with these cultures that are different than our own? With an Asian culture; with the Muslim cultures around the world— over a billion Muslims around the world; with the culture of China, which is different than ours; the culture of Southeast Asia, which is different than ours; the culture of Myanmar?

They're all human. They all have the same ultimate requirements, the same needs. But, they're different cultures. They think differently. They respond to different predicates than we respond to. But, we must have peaceful cooperation with these people, to solve world problems.

Then you start thinking about someone like Martin. And I want to indicate, in the context I just stated, what the significance of Martin is, today...."

**Speed:** That's how a President speaks to citizens of the United States, and that's what Lyn was doing in 2004, during his last campaign. Because Lyn understood Martin Luther King as part of the American Presidential system, just as Lyndon LaRouche has been for many decades now.

"What, Really, Are the Labor Committees?" is a document that Lyndon LaRouche wrote in 1977. I'm going to quote from it. It will surprise some of you, but that of course is kind of the point of today.

At the beginning of that particular section of this document, he wrote:

"The Labor Committees"—which was the original organization of young people that joined Lyndon LaRouche—"are a cadre association of political and physical scientists, modeled significantly in fact, upon the networks of Freemasons associated with Benjamin Franklin, during the last half of the 18th century, an association with the same fundamental world-outlook and objectives as Benjamin Franklin and his associates."

Later in that same document we find: "Not only was Benjamin Franklin widely acclaimed as the father of electricity, he was generally regarded by humanists as the organizer of human society, as the German intellect Johann Gottfried Herder wrote of him during that time."

"In a meaningful sense ... Ludwig van Beethoven can be considered the leading American composer. During Beethoven's youth in Bonn, Franklin's influence was notable in the university at Bonn, which was a hotbed of German republican humanism. Franklin's autobiography was a major intellectual influence among German humanist circles. During the last years of his life, the composer Wolfgang Amadeus Mozart was under the influence of Franklin's ideas, apart from his composing one, rather known, minor composition for the musical instrument, the glass harmonica, which amateur composer Benjamin Franklin had invented.

"More directly on Beethoven, there is conclusive evidence that the final movement of Beethoven's *Ninth Symphony*, is dedicated, in fact, to Benjamin Franklin."

So, that's Lyndon LaRouche. And that's why many of us have associated with Lyndon LaRouche for as long as we have been, proud to be associated. Shocking, new ideas about creativity, *changing* the view that people have of how they think things are.

## The Long Arc of History

In 1978, Lyn wrote for the *Campaigner* magazine, "The Secrets Known Only to the Inner Elites," in which he documented that the real war in Western civilization for a 2,500-year period, was between Plato, seen on the left, and Aristotle, on the right, between the concept of humanism based on the idea of scientific and artistic creativity as the birthright of every individual, and the opposing idea that people are to be subjugated, that there are different species, there are different "races," and that some are superior to others.

Lyn described what he called the "machine-tool principle." This was part of his revolution in econom-

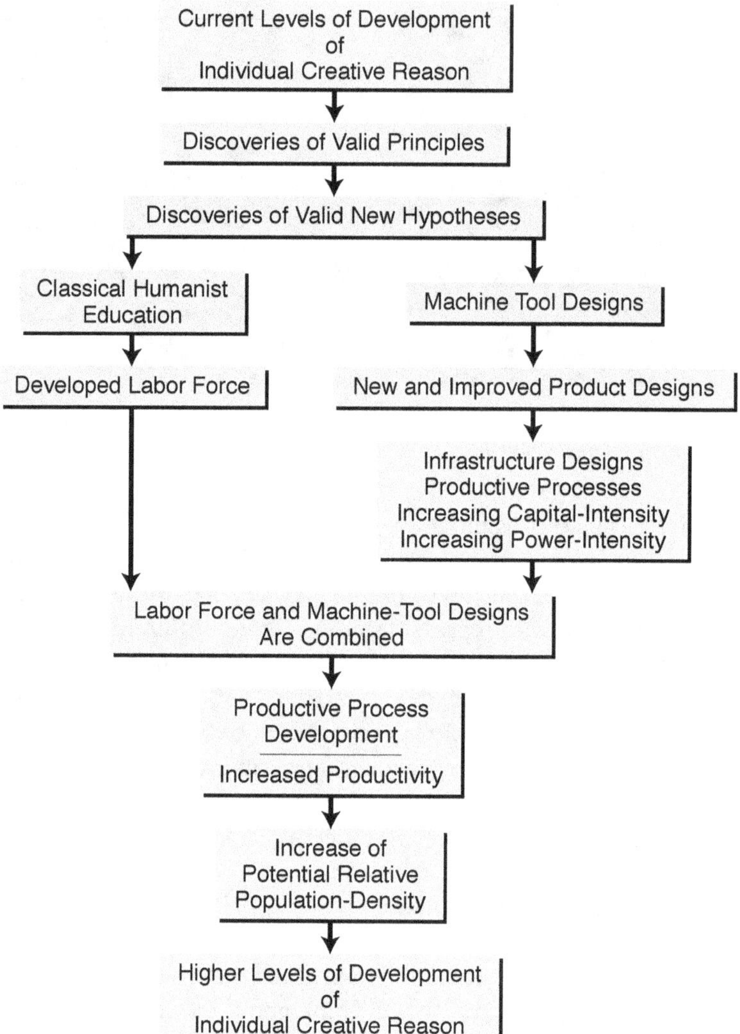



ics, to give the idea of how you move from a conception—how creativity becomes productivity. And this idea, that you take the current level of development of human reason, and by creating a discovery of a valid hypothesis, and by applying that through experiment, repeatable experiment, to the human mind as a whole, humanity is uplifted by generating new conceptions never before existent in the universe; and that that is the basis of productivity, and that is the basis of economic progress.

This form of machine-tool principle, when used properly by a society, develops levels of human productivity and capability which are expressed in what Lyn has called "potential relative population density increase." That is, not merely the number of people in-

Dennis Speed

*Two examples of the use of machine tools: Space Shuttle control panel (left) that exemplifies LaRouche's application of the machine-tool principle and (right) the final ignominious conclusion of the baby-boomer generation.*

creases, but the number of people at a higher standard of living increases, in greater concentrations, per square unit area.

The world is therefore not only not overpopulated, the world *needs* more people. If, for example, if the United States had 3 or 4 billion people, it still wouldn't be overpopulated. China has 1.5 billion people and is not overpopulated. But *that* idea, about which of course we heard Barack Obama say something to the Africans, is *exactly* the opposite of the current, popular idea of the entirety, nearly, of American culture today. Go out on the street, and you ask people, particularly as they watch the homeless and so on, that are right outside this hotel, whether they think the United States needs more people, and you know the visceral response you'll get.

*That* is the product of British ideology and of the domination of the American mind by Aristotelian thinking. So, now instead of *that* application of the machine-tool principle as exemplified by the control panel of the Space Shuttle, we have its strange modern incarnation seen driven on the streets of New York by an aging baby boomer.

The space shuttle control panel exemplifies LaRouche's application of machine tools. This modern incarnation is something a lot of the younger people know all about. That photo is the final, ignominious conclusion of the baby-boomer generation. [laughter] I took that picture about two days ago, sitting in my car, being assaulted by a lot of noise outside, and I turned around and somebody was playing AC/DC or a similar cacophony.

In order to relieve you all of that unseemly sight, we're going back to Lyn. Let's go to Kempinski Hotel Bristol Berlin. Lyn's ability to use his conception of creativity to forecast, is the primary thing that distinguishes him from every other economist alive. And we're going to give you an excerpt from that 1988 speech at the Kempinski in Germany.

**Lyndon LaRouche:** Many today will agree, that the time has come for early steps toward the reunification of Germany, with the obvious prospect that Berlin might resume its role as the nation's capital.

For the United States, as for Germans, and for Europe generally, the question is, will this reunification process be brought about by assimilating the Federal Republic into the East bloc's economy, or economic range of influence, or can it be accomplished in a different way? In other words, is a united Germany to come into being as a part of Europe from the Atlantic to the Urals, as President de Gaulle proposed, or, as Mr. Gorbachov has desired, a Europe from the Urals to the Atlantic?

**Speed:** That press conference took place on Columbus Day, 1988. The Berlin Wall was up. There

# 'We Must Build a Bridge From Hell to Purgatory'

## Lyndon LaRouche Addresses the Schiller Institute Labor Day Conference

*American economist Lyndon LaRouche delivered the keynote to the Labor Day conference of the Schiller Institute/International Caucus of Labor Committees, in Vienna, Virginia, Sept. 3. The text of his presentation follows.*

Today, what I'm going to do, should not be properly classified as an address, but as a *long briefing*, because this is in the nature of a report, and my effort to give you, with the aid of some other material available, a briefing on the most important issue, the most important fight, the most important opportunity which exists for every nation and for every individual person in the world today. The fight which I'm going to outline to you, is the only fight worth fighting. No other issue is important, because all of the impor-

By disintegration, I mean a process which is like a chemical explosion, but this one will resemble more a thermonuclear explosion of some hundred megatons. It starts with what the Russians call a Kolmogorov equation, when reverse leverage applied to an international financial bubble, begins to act, and you get a chain reaction, an explosion. One morning the banking system is there, the market systems are there, and within 24 hours or 72 hours at the most, the entire world banking system, the financial system, the monetary system, has not merely collapsed, it has disintegrated, in the sense that the bank does not function any more, the monetary system does not function any more.

Terms of trade no longer exist; payments among national and international institutions, private and public, no longer

was a Soviet Union. All those things existed. But Lyndon LaRouche gave a speech that was later made into a nationally televised broadcast, as part of his Presidential campaign—we placed that speech on nationwide U.S. television. In it he forecast the unification of Germany, a year before the Berlin Wall fell, and two years before that re-unification occurred. *How* did he do it?

The document, "We Must Build a Bridge from Hell to Purgatory, as a 650-Year Historical Cycle Ends," is a transcript of the keynote speech delivered by Lyn at a Schiller Institute conference in 1994. At a different times, we have talked about Lyn's conception of economics, and Lyn's approach to it. At different times, we have talked about what made him a unique figure. But it was the looking at history in arcs, large-scale cycles, that allowed him to actually see, not merely, "predict the future." For Lyn, the idea that the future determines the present, *is* this conception of history. Earlier today, Helga referenced his book, *Earth's Next Fifty Years*. That book is right now unfolding: It's the template of what is unfolding in our time. It also is the guide for our organization now, as to what it is we intend to see happen, as we cause the

Presidency today to realize what Lyn was trying to do, in his several Presidential runs, and in particular in his Presidential runs of the period from 1988 until 2004.

### Forecasting as a Creative Act

In 1975, the first kernel of what today is called the World Land-Bridge was proposed by Lyn after a return from Iraq. In April 1975, he proposed what he called the International Development Bank. The pamphlet, "How the International Development Bank Will Work," priced at $1, was gotten out in hundreds of thousands of copies by our organizers, directly to the American people. That meant going to plant gates, to unemployment centers, to street intersections and to airports, and organizing the American people around the seed-crystal of what you now see that has evolved in Asia.

LaRouche's 1990 Oasis Plan, the plan for Southwest Asia (also called the Middle East), was a proposal that he was working on at the same time as his International Development Bank proposal. It's not well known by a lot of people. We issued a pamphlet titled, "Secure World Peace with Economic Development: Implement LaRouche's Oasis and Productive Triangle Programs." The idea of the Productive Triangle, which then became the Eurasian Land-Bridge, and then became the New Silk Road, and later the World Land-Bridge—that idea was evolved by Lyn, while in jail: He went to jail because of his successful organizing of the American Presidency in 1983.

And so, sitting in jail, and hearing the news about the Berlin Wall falling, his response was to formulate *this* conception, called the Productive Triangle, and to have us, as an organization, with Helga Zepp-LaRouche leading that organizing—go out and organize on a plan that he literally created out of his head, in a jail cell!

We have in our presence, as an

economist, like it or not, a genius, whose ability to forecast was based on a creative method, a conception that he has demanded that an organization of his associates replicate.

He has not been an armchair intellectual, as I think people know. Lyn is highly combative. And we'd like to now show you something that some of you will know, but for those of you who don't, the following is from a webcast from July 25, 2007—*before* the famous collapse of markets and so forth and the housing bubble.

**Lyndon LaRouche:** There *is* no possibility of a non-collapse of the present financial system—none! It's finished, *now*! The present financial system can not continue to exist *under any circumstances, under any Presidency, under any leadership, or any leadership of nations*. Only a fundamental and sudden change in the world monetary financial system will prevent a general, immediate chain-reaction type of collapse. At what speed we don't know, but it will go on, and it will be *unstoppable*! And the longer it goes on before coming to an end, the worse things will get.



Schiller Institute

*Lyndon LaRouche presenting his "Typical Collapse Function" in 1996. When the Financial and Monetary Aggregates curves cross, a physical economic breakdown occurs.*

**Speed:** Now, that was not news that Lyn had not tried to deliver, and warned people about, much earlier.

In 1995, his famous Triple Curve (Typical Collapse Function) had described this process in geometric terms, in which the idea was that as less and less investment is made into the physical well-being of the economy, combined with an out-of-control Casino Mondial—developing with derivatives and so on—a point of inflection will be reached. You see there at the top of the chart, the the curves for the financial aggregates and the monetary aggregates have crossed. It is at that point that a condition of physical economic breakdown in our economy is created. So that when Lyn delivered his 2007 forecast, this was something that had already been preceded by twelve years of warning people about what was going to occur.

It's also relevant that the year after his Triple Curve first appeared in 1995, Helga Zepp-LaRouche spoke at a conference in China, in June of 1996, on the New Silk Road. We did not simply, Cassandra-like, predict disaster. We moved to create something different—creativity instead of tragedy, and that's been basically the idea throughout.

In 1997, *Executive Intelligence Review* published a special report, "The True Story Behind the Fall of the House of Windsor." It may have seemed like a long time

Now Only LaRouche's Methods Will Work   37

coming, but what we reported then is exactly what you're living through now. That report (augmented by the recent reports that we've been releasing), tells the story of what is about to occur to the British Empire. It doesn't mean that it didn't occur back when we wrote it: It simply is the case that with much of what *Executive Intelligence Review* and the Schiller Institute do, using Lyndon LaRouche's method, is to present things that often become manifest later, though conceived earlier, because actually, that's the real impulse of history. When you're thinking about the future, when you're trying to actually conceptualize where mankind is to go, you seem to be speaking before events. But the truth of the matter is that most people, having been inundated with British ideology, don't see the present.

For example, today's present is what you see in China; but actually, today's present more importantly is what you read, if you read Lyn's *Earth's Next Fifty Years*. That is to say, that the colonization of the Moon, the mining of helium-3 on the Moon, the development of the African continent—so that what we have in Africa is perhaps millions of people who are possessed of the kind of genius of a Mozart, of a Beethoven. *That* is the reality of the present.

Lyn's fight to establish, or re-establish I should say, the American Presidency in that image, has been the dominant characteristic of his economics and of his fight in the United States.

## What Each of Us Can Do

Here is another excerpt from LaRouche's Talladega speech:

**Lyndon LaRouche:** It wasn't just that he [Martin Luther King] was a man of God: It's that he rose to the fuller appreciation of what that meant. Obviously, the image for him was Christ, and the Passion and Crucifixion of Jesus Christ. That was his source of strength. He lived that. He had gone to the mountaintop, at a point that he knew his life was threatened by powerful forces

in the United States. And he said, "I will not shrink from this mission, even if they kill me." Just as Christ said, and I'm sure that was in Martin's mind, at that point. The Passion and Crucifixion of Christ is the image which is the essence of Christianity. It's an image, for example, in Germany, or elsewhere, where the Bach *St. Matthew Passion* is performed. It's a two-hour performance, approximately. In those two hours, the audience, the congregation, the singers, the musicians, re-live, in a powerful way, the Passion and Crucifixion of Christ. And this has always been important: *To re-live that.* To capture the *essence* of what Christ means, for all Christians. And Martin showed that.

The difference is this—and I'll come back to Jeanne d'Arc (or Joan of Arc, in English). The difference is, most people tend to believe, "Yes, I wish to go to Heaven," or something like that. Or, don't. Don't care. But, they are looking for answers within the bounds of their mortal life. They're thinking of the satisfactions of the flesh. The security they will enjoy, between the bounds of birth and death. Whereas, the great leader, like Martin, rises to a higher level. They think of their life, as the Gospel presents it, as a "talent." That is, life is a talent, given to you: You're born, and you die. That is your talent, what you have in that period. The question is, you're going to spend it anyway. *How* are you going to spend it? What are you going to spend it to secure for all eternity? What are you going to do, as a mission, that will earn you the place you want to occupy in eternity?

Martin had a clear sense of that. That mountaintop address, for me, struck me years ago—*clear*: It was just a clear understanding of exactly what he was saying; what he was saying to others. Life is a talent: It is not what you get out of life; it's what you put into it that counts.

**Speed:** There's a famous passage from King that people know, and we're only going to refer to it here. The passage is:

"Like anybody, I would like to live a long life. Longevity has its place. But I'm not concerned about that now. I just want to do God's will. And He's allowed me to go up to the mountain. And I've looked over. And I've seen the Promised Land. I may not get there with you. But I want you to know tonight, that we, as a people, will get to the Promised Land!

"And I'm happy, tonight. I'm not worried about anything. I'm not fearing any man. Mine eyes have seen the glory of the coming of the Lord."

*That* is Lyndon LaRouche's economics, stated by Lyndon LaRouche in *his* way, as King expressed that principle in his way.

What's important is that, as we, this week, consider the tragedy of 1968, we consider that tragedy only as embedded within the creativity that takes us from 2018 to 2068—the next fifty years. To see it, in other words as an inflection point in that 2,500-year battle between the Platonists and the Aristotelians, and to recognize that, in our time, and in our presence, has dwelt an individual, who has personified for all of us, what each of us can do, if we make ourselves an instrument of history, that can in fact create a new cultural paradigm and shift the world upward, from Hell to Purgatory, even, perhaps, Paradise. [applause]

JAMES GEORGE JATRAS

# The Urgency of a Trump-Putin Summit

*James George Jatras is a former U.S. diplomat and former adviser to the Republican Senate Leadership. This is his address to the Schiller Institute conference, "Dona Nobis Pacem—Grant Us Peace, Through Economic Development," convened in New York City on Saturday, June 9, 2018. He spoke on Panel 2 of the conference, titled "Choosing Creativity—Not Tragedy—In Economics and Statecraft."*

Schiller Institute

*James George Jatras*

Thank you, Mr. Speed. I appreciate your presentation. It greatly expanded my own understanding of where we really need to be thinking about going, positively, in the current global climate. Unfortunately, a lot of what I have to say, reflects more of what is going wrong in the current global climate, and the utter urgency of trying to do something about it. I thank the Schiller Institute for inviting me to make a few remarks here, today, and I really appreciate that my good friend, State Senator from Virginia Richard Black, will also be speaking today.

The topic I want to focus on is that there is a move, at long last, for a summit between President Donald Trump and President Vladimir Putin. This is absolutely essential. As we know, early in his Presidency, Mr. Trump did meet with his Chinese counterpart, President Xi Jinping, and that was a very positive development, but the broader international system, if it's going to have a positive stability, has to have three legs on the stool: And that's the United States, it's China, it's Russia. That's not to say other countries, Japan, India, Europe, don't matter, but without those three, we don't have anything approaching stability.

For various reasons, it's possible for the American President to meet with the Chinese President with no real problem. It hasn't been possible for Donald Trump to do that with Mr. Putin—not in the sense of a formal summit, but only in side-bar meetings at this or that international conference. That is not sufficient.

I think it's important to take a step back and describe why this is. But first, a few words about my own background. I'm a son of a career Air Force officer, a fighter pilot. The closest thing I have to a hometown is Bitburg Air Force Base in Germany. I'm the original Cold War baby, so to speak.

After I left law school, I served as a foreign service officer at the State Department, in what was then called the Office of Soviet Union Affairs—the Soviet desk. Interestingly, my father was the U.S. Air Force attaché in Moscow at the same time, so we saw the same U.S. government operations toward the Soviet Union during those days.

Unlike most other people at the time, I was convinced that it was quite possible we would see the emergence of a non-communist government in Moscow, in the fairly near future. I can tell you, nobody else at the State Department thought like that in those days. They simply assumed that communism and the Soviet Union was a forever phenomenon, and that we needed to reconcile ourselves to that "fact," whereas it occurred to me that a free, non-communist Russia was a distinct possibility and a desirable one.

In a rather naive way, I had a sense that if such a transformation were to happen in the Soviet Union, the great conflicts of the 20th Century would finally be over, and we would return to something like a non-ideological world, of peace and progress that existed before 1914. That didn't happen. And the reason it didn't happen, wasn't so much about the Russians. It was unfortunately about the nature of the people running our foreign policy establishment, here in the United States.

## They Want to Dismember Russia

I can remember when I was in Moscow for about a month in early 1993, as part of a parliamentary exchange between the U.S. Senate and the Russian Duma. People in Russia were not just pro-American: They were giddy pro-American. They were crazy pro-American. They were naively pro-American. And it is interesting the extent to which their pro-Americanism turned into a crashing disappointment, when we then expanded NATO in the mid-1990s, when we expanded it again, of course, in 2004, under the second Bush administration.

But I think one of the real clinchers was the Kosovo war in 1999. How many people in Russia would say to me, "We never believed anything the Soviet Union said about you. We knew it was all lies. But when we saw that, when we saw that NATO aggression, then we real-ized it was all true; that everything that the communists said about you was true." It was a real shot of cold water in the face, for them to feel that.

I think it was quite clear, that unfortunately, even though the Russian side had left the Cold War in the past, they'd withdrawn their troops from Eastern Europe, and they said OK to German reunification; but the people running our government, and also—let's be honest, as I think this group well knows—in cahoots, with their friends over in the United Kingdom, and in some other countries as well, were more than happy to prosecute that Cold War further. The only Russia they could tolerate was, at best, a puppet regime, as we had in the 1990s under Boris Yeltsin. The more preferable route, as Zbigniew Brzezinski laid out, would be breakup of Russia into at least three smaller states that would be much more easily manageable.

It came as a real shock to that establishment, when Vladimir Putin became President, and he pursued a course that I would describe as enlightened national self-interest—not at all closing the door to cooperation with the Western countries, but realizing that something was terribly wrong, that Russia had to take steps to secure its own sovereignty and its own interests. I think this is also what, of course, led to the very close collaboration, now, between Russia and China, which is the essence of Eurasian integration, which of course the Washington establishment sees as a great and terrible threat, whereas it really should be seen as the bridge to a real, cooperative future, and the building of an integrated, global economic system that can benefit everyone.

That is not the vision that we find here in Washington.

## Trump vs. the Brit-Allied Establishment

This relates to something that Dennis said earlier, the place of the President in making policy—you only have to convince one man. As it happened, as we know, in 2016, there were populist rebellions in both the Republican and Democratic parties. The Democratic Party had Bernie Sanders, who was cut out of the action through foul means by the Democratic establishment. Donald Trump, through some alchemy that I don't think ever has been adequately explained, managed to beat the establishment in the Republican Party, and he made it very clear that he

*Russian President Vladimir Putin (left) and U.S. President Donald Trump meet on the sidelines of the G-20 Summit, July 7, 2017, in Hamburg, Germany.*



wanted to improve ties with Moscow. This was one of his number-one priorities.

And that is exactly the reason why so much of the establishment, especially in the GOP, has been fighting tooth and claw, to first keep him from taking office; secondly to neuter him and possibly remove him from office; but above all, to make sure he cannot take this step in reconciling with Russia, which is essential. When we look at some of these conflicts in Syria, Ukraine, many other places, it is clear we have to have U.S.-Russian cooperation. Sometimes people ask me, "Why don't we team up with Russia, where we have a common interest in fighting the global jihad terrorism, Islamic radicalism?" The short answer is, "Because for the last half-century, we have been using that very same terrorism as a tool, first against the Soviet Union and now against Russia. It really would mean America switching sides."

I hope we are close to that. I hope we've gotten to the point now with the collapse of the so-called Russia-gate narrative, the growth of what really is "Spygate"—the extent to which our government spies on people, inserts **agents provocateurs** into other people's business to try to pin criminal charges on them. I hope that that's becoming clear now, and that the door is finally opening, to where we can have some positive trajectory forward in U.S.-Russia relations.

So, as I say, there is a petition on the White House website. I hope people will sign it: https://petitions.whitehouse. gov/petition/president-donald-trump-should-hold-early-summit-russian-president-vladimir-Putin

I do think a Summit with Putin is something Trump wants to do. It's unfortunate that there's virtually nobody around him, whom he has appointed, who seems to share the same vision. You do wonder why he appoints people who do not agree with some of his fundamental positions. I have to take that as a sign that he is still very embattled, even here in Washington, with the swamp all around him and the swamp critters who would very much like to bring him down.

We also have to keep in mind that the establishment that has been fighting him the whole way, even if they seem to be losing ground, will not "go gentle into that good night." I think we have to be very concerned about some provocation somewhere, whether it's in Ukraine, or Syria—another phony chemical weapons attack, something of that sort; perhaps an offensive by Kiev against the Donbas. These people are capable of doing anything to try to bust this up, which is what Dennis pointed out.

I have to tell you, ever since I endorsed Donald Trump on March 6, 2016, I have been very concerned that these people always have one solution to a problem like that: Get rid of the man who's a problem. We saw this with Jack Kennedy, we saw it with Bobby Kennedy, we saw it with Martin Luther King. I am very concerned, I have to tell you, about Donald Trump's personal safety, because so much hangs on the fate of one man and what he can do.

We live in a very critical moment, not only in American history, but in terms of the fate of the history of the world, a very critical juncture right now. [applause]

# The Strategic Importance of Victory, Peace and Development in Syria

*This is the address of Virginia State Senator Richard Black to the Schiller Institute conference, "Dona Nobis Pacem—Grant Us Peace, Through Economic Development," convened in New York City on Saturday, June 9, 2018. He spoke on Panel 2 of the conference, titled "Choosing Creativity—Not Tragedy—In Economics and Statecraft."*

**Dennis Speed:** Many of you have heard our next speaker here before at some of our events, maybe one very hot and raucous occasion in September 2016. Richard Black, Virginia State Senator: "The Strategic Importance of Victory, Peace and Development in Syria."

**Sen. Richard Black:** How are you today? This is Senator Dick Black, and as Dennis Speed mentioned, I'm going to discuss the Syrian situation and of course, the importance of victory, of peace, and development there.

Before I begin, please understand that I'm not a pacifist. I served 32 years in uniform, and in Vietnam, I flew 269 combat missions as a Marine helicopter pilot, and I made 70 ground patrols as a forward air controller for the First Marine Regiment, and dropped over 1,000 bombs in support of Marine companies that were engaged in battle. Both of my radiomen died beside me, and I was wounded attacking enemy forces across the Hoi An River.

So no one really has a greater love, understanding and respect for our troops, than I have for those who have been sent off to fight the wars in the Middle East. They are carrying out the orders they received and I respect them for their gallantry.

To hear the news, you'd think the United States is facing imminent military threats from Russia, from Iran, or from China. Just any day, there's going to be

*Richard Black, Virginia State Senator.*

some sort of an attack from somebody. But to be honest, in the near term, the threat from those nations is roughly *zero*. Our most pressing national security threat is the one that we ourselves have created: It's one that's posed by our own support of terrorist forces in Syria, and by the unlawful occupation of the sovereign territory of Syria. In short, the United States is engaged in a suicidal mission in Syria that literally threatens to destroy Western civilization itself.

Who could possibly imagine that Syria, a modest nation of just 23 million people, could be winning a war of aggression that has been waged against it for seven years, by a coalition of nations representing two-thirds of the world's military and industrial power? Think of that for a moment: One small nation, standing up, resisting the power of two-thirds of the world's military-industrial power.

But, Syria has unity of command, and they're supported by the Syrian people. On the other hand, the terrorists that we have supported are fractious. They're plagued by infighting, by greed, by hatred, by jealousy. The Syrian rebels lack the moral high ground. Now, in seven years of war, the West has been unable to groom one, single terrorist who has widespread popularity among the Syrian people.

Also, who could possibly have imagined that a few dozen key activists across the globe, and organizations like the Schiller Institute and the *Executive Intelligence Review*, could blunt the untold billions that have been dumped into Syria by the CIA, by MI6, and a dozen other intelligence agencies, in order to topple the Syrian government. The propaganda of those intelligence agencies wasn't focussed on misleading hostile nations; it was focussed on deceiving our own people about the realities of what was going on in Syria. However, we've had truth on our side, and truth, dissemi-

U.S. military forces in southern Syria, November 2017.



nated by social media, has gradually overwhelmed the lies, the deceit, and the covert actions sponsored by those intelligence agencies.

Let me take you back just a little bit: Before the Syrian war began, Syria was among the safest countries on Earth. It had endured forty years of peace with Israel. It wasn't perfect, but, look, neither are we! Syria had a well-balanced economy; it was debt free; it was not beholden to the IMF. It produced its own food, its own clothing, its own energy; it was rather self-sufficient, but engaged in active trade with other nations.

Syria had the greatest religious freedom and its women the greatest rights of any Arab country. Fifty-one percent of its college graduates were women, and those women could drive, they could dress in modern clothing, they could travel or do whatever they wanted without some man's permission. They were able to marry, they owned businesses, they had property. Their freedoms were light-years beyond those of our barbaric "coalition" allies Qatar and Saudi Arabia.

## Will This Barbarism Engulf the World?

But for seven years, the United States, Great Britain, France, and their allies, have actively worked to topple the legitimate, duly elected govern-

Muammar Qaddafi at African Union Summit, 2009.



ment of Syria, the one that was chosen through elections by the Syrians themselves. We have sought to replace it with an al-Qaeda-linked puppet government.

This isn't speculation. Gen. Wesley Clark, the former Supreme Allied Commander of Europe, reported that in 2001 he was present in the Pentagon when the Secretary of Defense had sent down orders to draft plans to overthrow seven nations in the Middle East. Among those seven were: Iraq, Libya, Syria, Yemen and Iran. Years later, WikiLeaks published secret plans developed by the chargé d'affaires at the U.S. Embassy in Damascus in 2006. Those plans provided a detailed outline of how the United States and its allies would destabilize and overthrow the legitimate Syrian government.

We executed that plan by creating religious divisions that led to an explosion of religious terror unprecedented in modern times. It's kind of like the story of Pandora's Box: You can unleash all of the hideous creatures in Pandora's Box in order to sic them on your enemy; but once they have been unleashed there is no controlling them. Since then, those creatures have turned on us, and they literally threaten our own destruction.

The United States has repeatedly attacked nations that did nothing hostile towards us. We had the First Gulf War against Iraq; we had the 2003 invasion of Iraq; we attacked Libya and subsequently murdered Muammar Qaddafi. Even though he offered to leave Libya and totally surrender the place, the decision was made among the United States, France, and Great Britain, that, honestly, Qaddafi knew too much and it would be better if he were simply murdered in Libya, and that's what was done. I understand that it was the French that actually orchestrated the incredibly vicious murder of Qaddafi.

We went on and launched a covert war on Syria, and today, we're not only fighting in Syria, but we are actively backing Saudi Arabia's very cruel war against the poverty-stricken people of Yemen.

We all remember when President Obama solemnly pledged that there

Aleppo, Syria, December 2016.

cc/Mil.ru

would be no "boots on the ground" in Syria. Today, American armed forces occupy almost a third of Syria. We have, conservatively, fourteen bases and airfields manned by American ground troops. There are, according to one American general who had a slip of the tongue, at least 4,000 uniformed GIs, and perhaps 2,000 contractors—sort of Blackwater-style mercenaries—who are stationed there. So much for the "no boots on the ground" promise that we were made.

President Trump told the American public, "I'm going to fight ISIS and I'm getting us out of there." It wasn't a week before his staff contradicted him, saying "No, we're not leaving Syria. We're going to stay there permanently; we have other things to achieve."

But here's the good news: Syria and its allies are winning the war! Now, why is that important to the United States, which has fought to defeat Syria for seven years? The reason is that Syria is the center of gravity in the war on terror. I attended the Army War College, the Command and General Staff College. They taught us that in military terms the center of gravity is that objective which determines the outcome of a struggle. In this case, it is Syria that will determine whether civilization survives, or whether barbarism surges forward and potentially engulfs the world.

Were Syria to fall, Lebanon and Jordan would almost certainly collapse in short order. That epic jihadist victory would create a massive, massive jihadist army, and the radicalization of the Syrian caliphate would probably incentivize Turkey, which has already moved in a distinctly violent, jihadist direction, to embark on a final showdown with Europe.

## U.S. Support for al-Qaeda and ISIS

From the outset of the seven-year Syrian war, the legitimate, UN-recognized government of President Bashar al-Assad has faced bands of savage terrorists. I want you think for a moment about those terrorists, and to re-alize—we have called them "rebels," we've called them "opposition," we've called them "moderate rebels." The fact is, that virtually every single one of those opposition groups has fought shoulder to shoulder in alliance with al-Qaeda at various times.

Now for those of you listening, who are perhaps a bit younger, it's very important to recall that al-Qaeda were the terrorists who hijacked four passenger planes on September 11, 2001 and used them to attack the Pentagon and the Twin Towers. They killed 3,000 Americans, and in the Twin Towers, Americans were forced to the top of the towers where they faced the choice of either dying in a ball of flames, or leaping to their deaths. Literally hundreds of American citizens leaped a quarter of a mile from the height of the Twin Towers to where they splattered on the sidewalks of New York.

I think that Americans would be *stunned* were they to realize that we had sided with that same al-Qaeda and with its allies throughout this war. We have armed, we have recruited, we have trained, and we have paid jihadists, through the CIA's top secret Project Timber Sycamore, which was discovered and subsequently abandoned by the U.S. government, and through other secret projects. But there's no doubt that there are other

VOA/Almigdad Mojalli

*Sana'a, Yemen in October, 2015, months after an airstrike.*

programs that are underway to make sure that the terrorists have an abundant supply of weapons, ammunition, financing, whatever they need. We have never stopped siding with the terrorists from literally Day 1 of the war.

If America were to switch sides or, more practically, if we simply abandoned the effort to impose a puppet regime on Damascus, that war would end quickly. This entire effort against Syria began when we invaded Libya for the purpose of plundering its stores of arms and munitions. We sent those arms and munitions through Turkey and on to Syria, where, according to a secret study conducted by the Defense Intelligence Agency in 2013, the Central Intelligence Agency distributed those arms—advanced arms, I'm not just talking about bullets, I'm talking about tanks, artillery, TOW anti-aircraft missiles, or antitank missiles, and things of that sort. We distributed all of those things, indiscriminately to all rebel groups. And the Defense Intelligence Agency reported that the rebels that received them, specifically included al-Qaeda and ISIS.

America established a huge coalition, ostensibly to fight ISIS. However, it's rather curious that the coalition declined to interdict the main source of ISIS income, which was plundered Syrian oil. ISIS has garnered income from many places. They did it through kidnapping; they did it by killing Yazidi and Christian children and harvesting their organs and selling them on the open market. They plundered the ancient antiquities of Palmyra and they sold them off. But the biggest source of ISIS income was a fleet of 2,000 oil tanker trucks. Full of stolen Syrian oil, they ran them in long lines that were waved across the Turkish border, across super-highways without interference.

And by the year 2014, the terrorists were driving back Syria's Army; there was every indication that unless something changed, the terrorists would seize Damascus, and vastly increase the ISIS-controlled territory. And the United States was supplying the tanks, the artillery, and so forth.

In 2015, however, the Russians sent a modest expeditionary force of several squadrons to help Syria. In two days, the Russians somehow managed to discover the ISIS oil tankers that we had deliberately overlooked for years. In two days, they destroyed 500 of those oil tankers, forcing ISIS to cut their soldiers' pay in half!

There have been a tremendous number of great victories by the Syrian government, the greatest being the liberation of Aleppo, followed by the elimination of

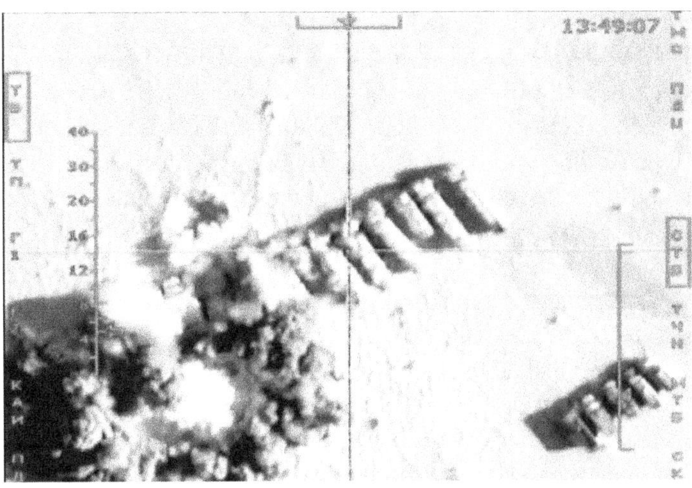

youtube/Russian Ministry of Defense

*Russian air force destroying truck convoy transporting oil for terrorists in Syria.*

major jihadist pockets within Damascus itself, so that today the Syrian government controls the territory holding about 90% of Syria's population, the terrorists being confined to two large pockets and several smaller ones.

## Trump Blackmailed

However, the biggest impediment to peace is not the terrorists. The terrorists are defeated, they are on the run. The biggest impediment to peace is America's occupation of 30% of Syria, and Turkey's occupation of a smaller part.

I want you to listen to something for just a minute, and I want you to absorb this: Isn't it ironic that the U.S. military unlawfully occupies in Syria, roughly twice the extent of territory compared to Russia's legitimate occupation of Crimea? How many times have you heard Europe just going ballistic over Russia moving into Crimea, which traditionally was Russian territory? And how many times have you heard the mainstream media protest the unlawful U.S. occupation of an area of Syria which is twice the size of Crimea? And we have done it with vastly more violence. In fact, when Russia moved into Crimea, the Crimeans welcomed them with open arms. There were no bullets fired, there were no people killed. The Russians simply moved back into what was traditionally Russia. We, on the other hand, have bombed and slaughtered and killed a great number of people in northeastern Syria.

President Trump's involvement in all of this is very interesting, because he twice expressed his intention to withdraw from Syria, and twice his pronouncements were *immediately* followed by false-flag gas attacks, that were actually staged by terrorist forces.

The deep state has effectively blackmailed Trump, holding him hostage though these covert actions that played off the totally fictitious Russian collusion narrative. We know today that there was no Russian collusion [in the 2016 U.S. elections]; I don't think anybody seriously even claims that there was Russian collusion, and yet, through all of the propaganda, every time there is a false flag gas attack, if President Trump delays for a moment to reflect on the veracity of terrorist reports that there had just been gas attack, he's accused of growing "soft on Russia." And in this way, the sinister forces of the deep state have managed to retain their dominance over American policy, and to continue to support terror in Syria.

Now the good news is that President Assad and the Syrian people are winning in Syria and that Syria will soon control all of Syria that's not under occupation by the United States and Turkey.

Now, I'll tell you that the coalition composed of the United States, Great Britain, France, Turkey, Qatar and Saudi Arabia, has done *enormous* damage to the infrastructure of Syria. Our occupation of northeast Syria seeks to rob that nation of much of its oil, natural gas, and agricultural production. That occupation ensures the impoverishment of Syria. We do it in order to establish this highly unstable, race-based, Kurdish state, in which the Kurds would dominate a majority of Arabs who occupy northeast Syria. It is one of these goofy, Western-style imposition of maps on the Middle East that have caused no end of problems, and we are certainly creating the worst possible map now. It's forcing us to permanently station American troops in order to suppress the Arab majority and keep them under the domination of the Kurdish minority in northeast Syria.

American withdrawal from Syria is vital. If we were to do that, we would achieve peace and security. The nation of Syria is able to care for its own population, its own borders; it's able to negotiate peace. They understand the culture in a way that Americans, in hundreds of years, *never* will.

## Bombs and Bullets, or Schools and Industry?

The good news is that rebuilding has already begun, although the rebuilding is inhibited to some extent by an American blockade of Syria, and by the fact that we have imposed banking sanctions that prevent the people from receiving food and medical supplies from Western countries. The United States has estimated that rebuilding Syria will cost a quarter-trillion dollars. Western countries have no interest in rebuilding what they have spent seven years to destroy.

Russia will help and Iran will help, but they simply don't have the funds for such a massive rebuilding of the country. However, China has already pledged considerable aid. They have teams of individuals who are scouring the country, looking for opportunities to rebuild infrastructure, and to re-create Syria in the great image that it once had.

I will tell you that from the many reports that I'm receiving, peace is returning to great regions of Syria today. We can expect that as areas become secured, reconstruction efforts will be led by China.

You know, it's a sad thing. I'm very proud of my country; I love my country, I've bled for my country, but the American paradigm, since the days, perhaps of Herbert Walker Bush and George Bush, the American paradigm has become bombs, bloodshed, reducing nations to rubble, and forcing them into submission. That's the American paradigm, and that is what we offer.

Today, we are in competition with the Chinese Silk Road paradigm. Their paradigm is funding infrastructure, reconstruction of what has been destroyed by the West; noninterference in nations' internal affairs, and peace. They don't come with bombs, they don't come with bloodshed, they come with roads, and dams, and schools, and industry.

I'm deeply concerned that over time, China's course will prevail and ours will inevitably crumble in the marketplace of ideas.

Peace in Syria will eventually return millions of refugees and diminish tensions throughout the Middle East. The return of peace will spill over to a diminution of global terror as Western powers recognize the bankruptcy of their failed strategy, and as we stop training, arming and recruiting violent jihadists from throughout the world and training them, literally on the battlefields of Syria, to go back to their home countries and destabilize those countries, and spread terror throughout the globe.

It is my very sincere hope, and my prayer, that the day will come when there will be forces that emerge in the Democratic and the Republican Parties in the United States, that world leaders will stop speaking in bellicose terms about how we're going to attack and how we're going to bully and how we're going to threaten other nations in the world. Perhaps, we're going to be able to hear world leaders speak of peace, once again.

Thank you very much.

# Qingdao SCO Meeting
# A Game-Changer for the Region

by William Jones

June 11—With two major international events taking place this past week, the G-7 in Charlevoix, Canada, and the 18th Summit of the Shanghai Cooperation Organization (SCO) in Qingdao, China, it was like a "tale of two cities," a theme popularized by Charles Dickens in his novel of that name. Indeed, it was the "worst of times" for the "old boys" in the G-7 and "the best of times" for the relatively new organization, the Shanghai Cooperation Organization, which also represents the interests of the developing countries. And the rancor expressed in the tumultuous aftermath of the Charlevoix G-7 strongly contrasted with the spirit of harmony, the "Shanghai Spirit" as it's called, which characterized the SCO meeting. And yet from these contrasting events, we can see new forms of "governance" emerging in the world, with President Trump—traveling to Charlevoix—calling for Russia's return to the G-7, in order to shake up this gaggle of politicians intent on preserving the geometry of the Cold War era, and President Putin replying from his press conference at the SCO that he would certainly be prepared to invite the leaders of the G-7 to Moscow for a G-8 Summit. While most of the G-7 leaders were fuming over President Trump's proposal, the new Italian Prime Minister Conte greeted it as a breath of fresh air. President Trump left the G-7 leaders stewing in their

PIB of India

*The Shanghai Cooperation Organization (SCO) Summit, in Qingdao, China, June 10, 2018.*

*Tajikistan President Emomali Rakhmon (left), Russian President Vladimir Putin (center), Chinese President Xi Jinping (second from right), and Kazakhstan President Nursultan Nazarbayev (right) at SCO Summit.*



own juices, in order to attend a meeting with North Korean leader Kim Jong-un for a major historic breakthrough in the 65-year-old "frozen conflict" on the Korean Peninsula.

The Shanghai Cooperation Organization was hosted this year by China and held in the beautiful Chinese coastal town of Qingdao, in Shandong Province, the home of the Chinese philosopher Confucius, whose spirit President Xi called forth as the guiding spirit of the SCO deliberations. The SCO was created in 2001, coming out of the 1996 meeting of five countries, China, Russia, Kazakhstan, Tajikistan, and Kyrgyzstan—the so-called "Shanghai Five"—to discuss border and border security problems remaining after the breakup of the Soviet Union. Uzbekistan joined the five in 2001 and the SCO was born. Their collaboration has since expanded into other areas and begun to attract more countries. At Qingdao, the now eight members, China, Kazakhstan, Kyrgyzstan, Russia, Tajikistan, and Uzbekistan, now including the new members India and Pakistan, discussed many of the regional issues, with an emphasis on how to push the economic development of the region forward, and how to combat an increasingly dangerous terrorist threat. In addition to the eight SCO members, there were also four observer nations at the meeting—Belarus, Iran, Afghanistan, and Mongolia. Also participating were six "dialogue partners"—Turkey, Sri Lanka, Nepal, Cambodia, Azerbaijan, and Armenia. Taking all of these into account, the SCO meeting had representation from countries representing over 45% of the world's population and 70% of the Eurasian landmass.

Characteristic of the organization is what is called the "Shanghai Spirit," a spirit of cooperation that President Xi noted was characterized by "mutual trust, mutual respect, respect for diverse civilizations, and pursuit of shared development." The addition of India and Pakistan to the SCO, two countries which have long been at loggerheads, symbolizes the importance of that spirit in working together to cope with common problems. The SCO may well represent for them a crucial forum to resolve some of the outstanding issues between them.

Together with the BRICS (Brazil-Russia-India-China-South Africa) group, the SCO is one of the most important groupings representing the developing sector and its interests. At Qingdao, there was greater emphasis on the issues of development and on the need for improving the mechanisms of "global governance." Most of the countries involved in the SCO are also involved in the Belt and Road Initiative, and there is great synergy between the two. China proposed to create a special lending facility within the SCO Inter-Bank Consortium specifically for development projects in the SCO countries, and will itself contribute $4.7 billion to that facility. China also agreed to train 2,000 law enforcement officers from SCO countries for three years, to assist the SCO countries in law enforcement. In addition, China will provide 3,000 training opportunities in human resources development for SCO member states in the next three years, in order to enhance public understanding and support for the SCO.

Security continues to be a major issue of SCO concern, as do the increasing tensions on the international strategic level. The defeat of ISIS in Syria has not led to the complete destruction of that organization, but rather to the redeployment of their extant cadre to other nations of the world, including those in Central Asia as well as Southeast Asia, which have already felt some of the effects of this redeployment.

The issue of Afghanistan was also a major item of

discussion at the summit. President Emomali Rakhmon of Tajikistan called for a major infrastructure program for Afghanistan, particularly the construction of new roads and highways, in order to create greater connectivity within Afghanistan, and between Afghanistan and its neighbors, of which Tajikistan is one. President Xi praised the Tajik President's contribution to the discussion. The failure to get a handle on the insurgency in Afghanistan can easily spill over into its neighbors. This is all the more reason for the SCO members who live in the same neighborhood to play a greater role in dealing with the problems in Afghanistan. And while the SCO is concerned with security issues, and does conduct joint military maneuvers and could play a role in "peace missions," the SCO will probably not serve as a military force in Afghanistan to quell the insurgency. Still, the possibility offered by the SCO countries for greater economic and trade collaboration with Afghanistan can provide a crucial contribution to this unsettled nation—whose woes fundamentally stem from a total lack of economic development—and in that way contribute to a peaceful resolution of the conflict. If Belt and Road projects can be extended to Afghanistan, this would go a long way to quelling much of the discontent there, and create new possibilities for gainful employment for the Afghan people.

*Indian Prime Minister Narendra Modi (left), Russian President Vladimir Putin (center), and Chinese President Xi Jinping (right) at SCO Summit.*

The SCO meeting was also the opportunity for a series of important bilateral meetings between the leaders of these countries. Both Kazakh President Nursultan Nazarbayev and Russian President Vladimir Putin used the opportunity of the summit to pay official state visits to China during the course of their stay. China-Russia cooperation, in particular, is absolutely crucial for the SCO's development. The summit and President Putin's state visit have significantly strengthened the efforts by Russia and China to synchronize their respective individual regional development initiatives—the Belt and Road Initiative with Russia's Eurasian Economic Union (EAEU). On May 17, the two sides signed an agreement in Astana on trade and economic cooperation between the EAEU and China. "China and Russia are the main engines of the SCO," said Jiang Yi, deputy director of Russian studies at the Chinese Academy of Social Sciences, in an interview with *Global Times*, "and their cooperation will benefit regional and world stability." President Putin, during his state visit, had an opportunity to travel on China's high-speed rail between Beijing and Tianjin with President Xi. China is also in the process of constructing the first high-speed rail system in Russia between Moscow and Kazan, the first leg of a high-speed rail connection between the two countries.

There was also an important meeting between Indian Prime Minister Narendra Modi and China's President Xi, and another between Modi and Putin.

Chinese President Xi Jinping has proposed a new model of cooperation between countries, "a community of shared destiny for mankind." In many respects, the SCO and its "Shanghai Spirit" serve as a prototype for this type of community. And with the old forms of "world governance" such as the G-7 now coming apart at the seams, the new spirit of win-win cooperation now gaining ground in Asia can become the leading paradigm to bring the world out of its present crisis.

# Completely New Strategic Alignment in Asia Is Shaping the Future: Will the Foolish Europeans Be Left Behind?

*This is the edited transcript of the June 7, 2018 Schiller Institute New Paradigm webcast, an interview with the founder of the Schiller Institutes, Helga Zepp-LaRouche. She was interviewed by Harley Schlanger. A video of the webcast is available.*

**Harley Schlanger:** Hello. I'm Harley Schlanger from the Schiller Institute. Welcome to this week's international webcast featuring our founder and President, Helga Zepp-LaRouche.

As every week now, there are quite extraordinary developments, many of which have been shaped by what we've been talking about on this program, and what our Schiller Institute organization and allied forces in the LaRouche PAC have been doing internationally. One of those things was the publication of an important article by a leading Russian think tank, and Helga, why don't we start with that?

**Helga Zepp-LaRouche:** Yes. I would like to encourage you, our viewers, to read this article that was written by Harley Schlanger, who you see here with me on the program. It is was posted June 3 in the Experts Column on the front page of the website of the Russian International Affairs Council (RIAC), Russia's premiere academic and diplomatic think tank that has on its board of trustees a number of very important Russian personalities, including Foreign Minister Sergey Lavrov. Harley's article is titled, "No More Doubt: It's the U.K., not the Russians, that Meddled in the U.S. Elections."

The article presents the important news that it is now proven that it was the British secret services—GCHQ, MI6—and various other British institutions that meddled in the United States, as far back as 2015, and conducted a massive intervention into the Presi-

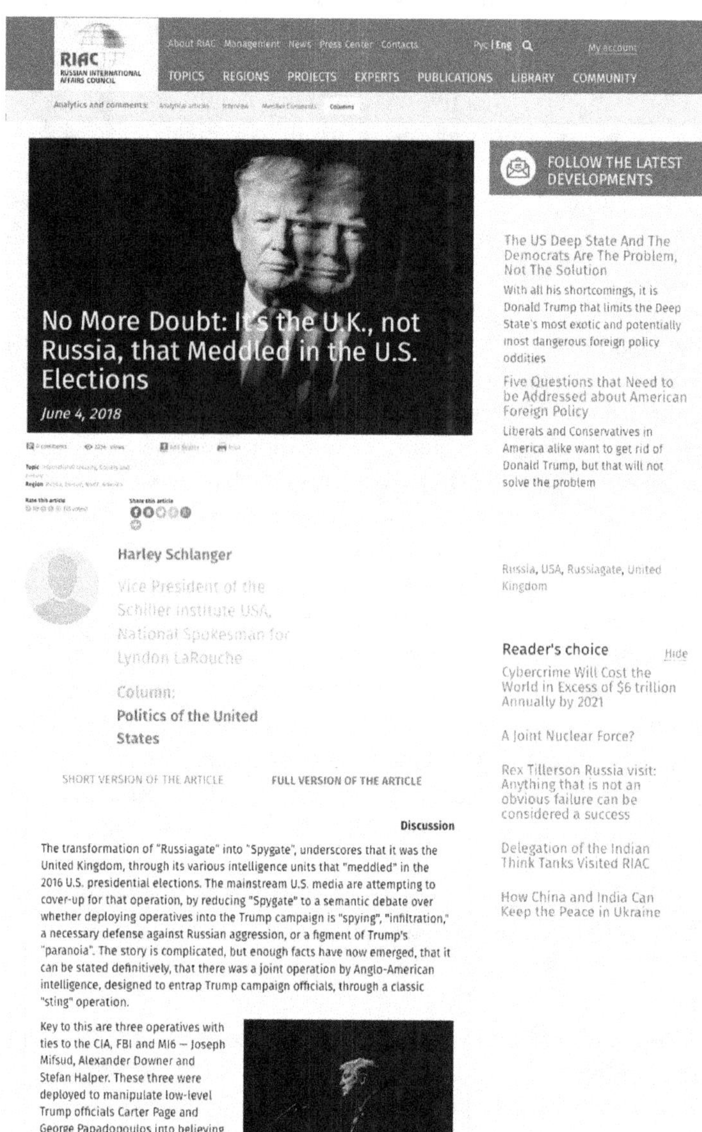


dential campaign in 2016, and further, following the election victory of President Trump, to create Russiagate.

It is quite important that the British role—which President Trump said could become the biggest scandal in the history of the United States—is being noted in such an authoritative publication in Russia. Russiagate has now interestingly turned into "Spygate."

I want to congratulate you, Harley. You did a good job. So, please do read Harley's article.

On April 19 of this year, Russia's Foreign Ministry spokeswoman, Maria Zakharova, briefed the international media on the history of various political crimes and intelligence operations by the British.

**Schlanger:** Thank you for that, Helga. A lot more will be coming out in the next days, when the Justice Department's Inspector General issues his report. Indications are that former FBI Director James Comey is going to be on the firing line; ditto for Andrew McCabe, Comey's deputy; more on FBI agent Peter Strzok. McCabe is actually asking for immunity to testify before the Senate.

As part of a Congressional investigation into the FBI's handling of the Hillary Clinton email affair, Strzok's boss, Bill Priestap, had an eight-hour, closed-door interview with members of the joint investigation group of the House Judiciary and Oversight Committee and Government Reform Committee. So I think there's going to be a lot more coming out on this, and I'm expecting more evidence to show that it was the British that meddled, and that they did so through individuals such as John Brennan and James Clapper. They're the ones on the firing line.

Last week, we were talking about the still unresolved situation in Italy. It seems to be somewhat resolved. A new government has been brought in, which has given the bureaucrats in Brussels quite a shock. So why don't you update us on what's happening in Italy?

**Zepp-LaRouche:** Very important changes are occurring. Yesterday, Prime Minister Giuseppe Conte's government was approved by the Italian Senate and the

Giuseppe Conte, Italian Prime Minister.



Chamber of Deputies. In his first speech, Conte announced that he is planning to cause a shift in the sanctions policy towards Russia; he also announced that the new government would go for banking separation. There has not been a lot of comment yet on the Glass-Steagall banking separation issue, but all kinds of people felt compelled to come out against getting rid of the sanctions. NATO Secretary General Jens Stoltenberg said, "Sanctions are important, until Russia changes its behavior," which is really incredible: What he means of course, is Crimea and similar things, but we have gone through that story: it was the West which caused the events in Ukraine to explode, and Crimea was only the 10th or 12th event in a long series of provocations coming from the West.

Kurt Volker, the former U.S. Ambassador to NATO and now U.S. Special Representative for Ukraine Negotiations, said Italy does not have the right to change the sanctions because the sanctions are EU law. That's really ludicrous, because this government was voted in, *because* they disagree with all of these policies, including the sanctions against Russia.

So it remains to be seen what will happen next.

Italy's new Minister of Economy and Finances, Giovanni Tria, has an excellent relationship with China and speaks fluent Chinese. His university had a model relationship with a Chinese university. Tria issued a paper, which we will have to analyze more closely, calling for more public investment, claiming that this can be done within the EU guidelines of rigorous budget rules and progressive government debt reduction. But, he says, the only way this can be done is by increasing public investment, and there is talk about possible use of some Italian banking institutions to do that.

This all looks very promising. It is also clear that the Italian people fully support this government. There were rallies over the weekend, where Conte, Salvini and Di Maio addressed large crowds of people. There was also some very useful advice from Professor Michele Geraci, a government advisor, that China can greatly help Italy with problems in Africa. Geraci underscored that China is investing in Africa, and that's what Italy should do along with China. That is the only way the refugee crisis can be solved in a human way.

These are very important changes. A very interesting situation is shaping up. There is now a new wind blowing in Europe, and the blatant intervention by the European Central Bank (ECB) is not helping the EU bureaucrats.

Two days ago the *Financial Times* had a very interesting article, showing with charts how the ECB, in the final phase of the attempt by Conte to form the first government with Paolo Savona as the economy and finance minister, had actually helped to increase the Italy-Germany 10-Year bond spread, by reducing the amount of Italian state bonds they were buying, and in this way signaled the speculators to speculate against the Italian bonds. The ECB presented a technical pretext for their actions, claiming that this occurred at the same time the German bonds reached maturity, therefore its financial means were exhausted. But this is completely bogus. The European Central Bank has always had flexibility in deciding when they do what.

This diversion from the truth is seen as another blatant example of intervention. And it gives new meaning to what EU Commissioner Oettinger had said, namely, that the "markets will teach the Italians how to vote." If the ECB is doing the job of the supposed market, it is quite outrageous. As for Oettinger, it shows you the arrogance of such

Schiller Institute

*Marco Zanni, Italian Member of the European Parliament, speaking at a Schiller Institute Conference in Berlin, 2016.*

people: He said the Italians should work more and be less "corrupt." Maybe we should be talking about corruption in the EU, in Luxembourg and other places.

So, it really shows, people in the rest of Europe, and maybe in the United States as well are really anti-Italian, and that has nothing to do with the Italian people, but it has everything to do with the amount of propaganda which is being blasted against Italy. The same thing happened not so long ago against Greece. Remember, the Italian people have a long history: Europe's Golden Renaissance was centered in Italy. Italian culture is one of the absolutely important cultural influences in Europe. There is no Europe without Italy.

Everyone should really stop and think this through: Is it not better for the Italians to try to change something when they have not experienced *any* growth from several of their governments in row; or should Italians behave like sheep—like the Germans, who for the most part are doing well but are still behaving like lambs going to the slaughterhouse, and are not doing anything to oppose the austerity policies coming from the Merkel government, policies which are clearly not in their interest?

So, I urge you to counter these prejudices: Look at how the Italian government is unfolding. There are clearly some problems; you can see that there are non-productive green policies there. However, these first steps, moving against the sanctions, for banking separation, and the different approach to the development of Africa—all of these things are very, very promising.

**Schlanger:** On that point, earlier today I spoke with Marco

CC/IU/P. Woods

*Günther Oettinger, European Commissioner for Budget and Human Resources.*

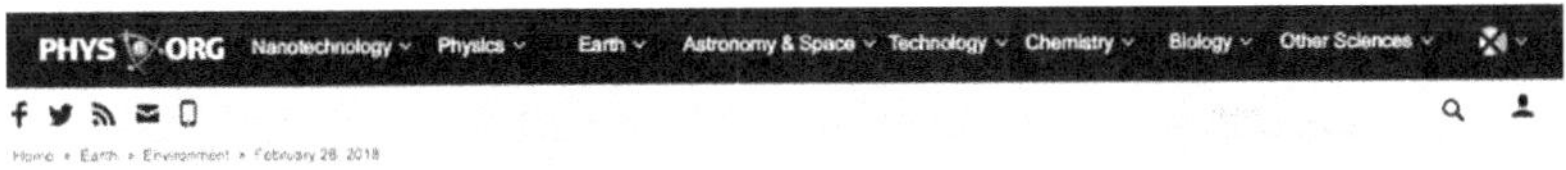

It sounds like something from Wakanda, the futuristic African kingdom of the hit movie "Black Panther".

Zanni, an independent Member of the European Parliament from Italy, who is very close to the leadership of the Lega, one of the two parties in the government coalition. He pointed out to me that three policies of the new Italian government are precisely the first three of Lyndon LaRouche's Four Laws: Glass-Steagall, a national bank to fund investments, and an emphasis on infrastructure.

He said something else very significant: He said he thinks that Salvini, the new deputy prime minister and the head of the Lega, will be going to China within a month or so; and a major focus for the Italians is to collaborate with China in Africa. He said that people often say that the Italian vote for the so-called "populists" was an anti-immigrant vote. Zanni said, "No, we're trying to find a solution to that problem by developing these nations." That's pretty much what has been proposed in the report by the Schiller Institute on the Near East and Africa policy, *Extending the New Silk Road to West Asia and Africa: A Vision of an Economic Renaissance*. Maybe you want to say something more on that.

**Zepp-LaRouche:** Yes, for sure. How can this problem be solved? By the year 2040, it's expected that there will be two billion Africans. If anyone thinks two billion people can be put in camps in Libya or in some other North African or other country, as it is being proposed by the EU right now, or that two billion Africans fleeing from hunger and epidemics can be kept out of Europe by increasing the coast guard and other such efforts to prevent people from crossing the Mediterranean, they are obviously delusional!

The only way to solve this absolutely terrible catastrophe of the refugee crisis, is with large-scale development of Africa. China has done a brilliant job. They have completely changed the outlook of the Africans, who have hope for the first time that they can overcome poverty and underdevelopment, now, with the help of China. One such program that we talked about some time earlier, is the Transaqua Project, an agreement to replenish Lake Chad, among the countries of the Lake Chad Basin region, plus China and Italy, as a model of how European countries can work together with China and African nations for large-scale infrastructure. Such programs are the necessary precondition for, and an essential part of, industrialization, and for development of agriculture, and productive jobs for all the young people who are already alive and those soon to be born in Africa.

It's a very good thing that Italy now has a changed policy outlook toward Africa. One of the reasons why the coalition of these two parties won the election, is that Italy was completely left to fend for itself by the EU Commission on the refugee crisis. Italy is now changing and seriously trying to work with China, but also Japan, and India. This is part of the growing phenomenon of many countries now being interested in investing in real industrialization in Africa. The best thing that could happen would be for more European nations, and the United States, to join hands in the New Silk Road approach towards Africa. That is what we are fighting for.

**Schlanger:** Another thing sending shock ways through Europe, is the visit by Russian President Vladimir Putin to Vienna, Austria this week, where he had very successful meetings with Chancellor Sebastian Kurz and President Alexander Van der Bellen. What's the significance of this Austrian trip by President Putin, Helga?

**Zepp-LaRouche:** It's very important, because all the efforts by the neo-liberal/neo-con mass media to demonize Putin and paint a picture as if he were completely isolated, has been proven completely wrong. He

*Russian President Vladimir Putin (left) and Chancellor of Austria Sebastian Kurz (right) giving a press conference following talks in Vienna, June 6, 2018.*



got an excellent reception in Vienna. Chancellor Kurz said he will also work towards overcoming the sanctions. Austria will be assuming the Presidency of the Council of the European Union for the second half of 2018 on July 1, so Kurz will have quite some means to initiate steps, especially since there is such a mood for change, in all the Visegrad countries [Slovakia, the Czech Republic, Hungary, and Poland], the East and Central European countries, the Balkan countries, and the Southern European countries, almost all of which are against the sanctions against Russia. So I can very easily see some room for change.

Putin was received with military honors and he gave a lengthy interview to the official Austrian TV channel, in which he commented on many issues. I think it was very important.

We were told by a very high-level contact that the EU had tried to do the same thing it had done in Italy—to not accept the new Austrian government, as they did with Italian President Mattarella this past May. But President Van der Bellen, according to this report, refused to bow to the pressure. In a certain sense, it's very ironic that Chancellor Kurz said, given that the EU is preaching so much about savings and austerity, that he—in his capacity as the new leader of the European Union—will dramatically work to cut costs in the EU bureaucracy—reducing the number of commissioners from 28 to 18, and closing down either Strasbourg or Brussels, because the EU spends EU200 million per year on deputies travelling between these two places, which he says is a complete waste that he wants to end.

So between Savona being the new European Affairs Minister in the Italian government, and the new Austrian approach, I think that there will be some important changes in the EU, and they may not be so pleasant for those who are trying to preserve the status quo.

**Schlanger:** We're seeing a shift underway toward Russia and also explicitly toward China from some of these countries. At the same time, at the EU summit, they're going to be talking about more militarization, more money, more forces for NATO. Do you think this is going to fly?

**Zepp-LaRouche:** Well, there is a major effort for increased militarization, both in NATO and in the EU. The Secretary General of NATO, Jens Stoltenberg, recently announced that they want to have a new NATO command in Ulm in Germany, and in Norfolk, Virginia, and a rapid deployment force for NATO, and a rapid deployment force for the EU. The Polish government wants to have a permanent base for one division of American troops. All of these proposals are clear-cut provocations, but against whom? Russia is not threatening anyone. The talk about Crimea is a pretext.

German Chancellor Merkel's suggestions that Europe has to become more independent from the United States because you can't rely on the United States any more, is part of the larger orchestration of a

*Jens Stoltenberg, NATO Secretary General.*

ridiculous narrative. Trump has demanded that all the Europeans should use 2% of their GDP on an increase in the cost of NATO, and that's what they're now doing. If Merkel wants to be serious, and wants more independence for Europe, the only way to do that in any meaningful way would be to do it together with Russia, and with China.

But the European NATO nations are not doing that. As a matter of fact, when Merkel was recently asked if it would be useful for Russia to return to the G8, she repeated the negative mantra, saying: "The annexation of Crimea was a flagrant violation of international law, and therefore Russia's exclusion from the G8 format was the right decision." If the European nations want to be serious, then they should admit Western complicity in the fascist coup in Ukraine, which was the trigger for all of these developments, including Crimea.

Xinhua

*Kim Jong-un, chairman of the Workers' Party of Korea (WPK) and chairman of the State Affairs Commission of the Democratic People's Republic of Korea (DPRK) in Singapore, June 10, 2018.*

We have not forgotten Victoria Nuland's bragging that the U.S. State Department under President Obama spent $5 billion on NGOs in Ukraine alone, for a color revolution and regime change. And many of the recipients of those funds belong to the Bandera pro-Nazi tradition. So, if you want to talk about "changing behavior," then the West should also change its behavior.

There is a complete double standard: Was the Iraq war based on justice and righteousness? Or was it based on lies? Did the Iraq war extinguish hundreds of thousands or more lives? What about the Libya war? If there is to be the same standard for everyone, then these wars should be put on the same level, but that is obviously not done.

I can only say it's a terrible thing that we have these war hawks in the West, while the rest of the world is moving in a completely different direction. The dynamic and spirit of the New Silk Road has already captured many countries in Europe. Hopefully those still on the warpath will soon recognize that their true self-interest is in cooperation, not confrontation.

**Schlanger:** One of those big changes coming up, apparently, will be from the summit next week between President Trump and Kim Jong-un of North Korea. This is part of this new dynamic in Asia. It does appear that this is going to take place; there's a lot of opposition coming from the United States, including from Democrats in the U.S. Senate, and Republicans, who are saying that Trump should not give anything to Kim Jong-un. Trump himself is saying he's going to go in with a somewhat flexible standard. I assume they will meet. What do you think is going to happen, Helga?

**Zepp-LaRouche:** We should remain alert until it really happens, because so often there are sabotage attempts in the last minute. I certainly see very good intentions coming from all of the participating nations, except from many Democrats in the United States, who are again proving themselves to be like they were with Obama, the war party. Concerning Trump, North Korea, China, South Korea, and Russia, all the signs indicate they really want to make this work.

There have been many delegations from the White House, from North Korea, in Singapore preparing for the summit; there was a statement by the South Korean President, Moon Jae-in, who said that he hopes a non-aggression pact can be included in the peace treaty between the North and the South. President Putin complimented Trump for his "courageous" idea of having this personal meeting, and promised that Russia would play an important role in the economic development of the North. Putin also said that there must be a 100% security guarantee for the North, so that the tragedy of Iraq and Libya is not repeated.

I think there are many reasons to be hopeful that this, indeed, will succeed. It will not be a one-time event. Russian Foreign Minister Sergey Lavrov has said that it has to be a very skillfully orchestrated series of events, in which mutual steps are being taken towards denuclearization, but also towards reducing and eventually eliminating the sanctions; and that the North Korean people need security guarantees and need to see the development of economic prosperity.

If these steps move forward with good intentions, there is great hope for success. One of the interesting indications of this process being on a pathway toward success is that the people of both South Korea and of North Korea are enthusiastic. Some observers think it will be almost impossible to reverse it, given the fact that the people of Korea are now very enthusiastic about this process succeeding.

If you look at the New Silk Road dynamic as the framework for this process, the reasons to believe that this can be a real success story are actually much better than in the case of the German reunification which took place under much worse geostrategic conditions, with Bush, Thatcher, and Mitterrand all determined to reduce the Soviet Union to an isolated Russia that would no longer be a superpower, but instead a raw-materials producing Third World country. The East of Germany was also the recipient of the full effect of this geopolitical insanity.

So I think the North Korea circumstances are actually much more favorable.

**Schlanger:** The picture you have just painted is part of this new strategic alignment that will be coming together next week in China, at a conference of the Shanghai Cooperation Organization. This also has the potential to not only push the Korean situation ahead, but the whole Silk Road process.

**Zepp-LaRouche:** Yes. I think we see clear signs that the efforts by the British, by the EU—which unfortunately was absolutely involved in this, and also previous U.S. administrations—to orchestrate India against China in the recent period, with Obama's so-called Asia pivot, which was the idea of the Indo-Pacific—meaning an alliance among Australia, Japan, India, and New Zealand, against China—does not function. There's a certain geopolitical faction in India, and they were playing on this

PIB of India

*Shri Narendra Modi, Prime Minister of India (right) meeting with Xi Jinping, President of China, in Wuhan, China, April 28, 2018.*

very heavily, saying India is the largest democracy in the world, and therefore should be on the side of the Western democracies, and not on the side of dirigistic China.

All this is now changing. There was the extremely important summit between India's Prime Minister Modi and Xi Jinping in Wuhan, where for two days the two leaders discussed all kinds of bilateral and multilateral issues. Modi's very important speech at the Shangri-La Dialogue in Singapore, was an important follow up. He not only referred to the more than 5,000-year history of India, and India's culture as being one of the greatest in human civilization, but he also spoke in terms of the one humanity of the future, much like the constant refrain of President Xi.

So there is a clear rapprochement between India and China. Both Modi and Xi stated that the two nations are the largest countries in the world, in terms of population, and if they work together, it will have a big, big impact on the entire world. And also, as we've discussed many times, India is moving toward cooperation with the New Silk Road.

I think there is a clear orientation toward an Asian Century, because the Asians are on a much better course right now. They are emphasizing innovation, science and technology, scientific progress as the source for the increase of production. They are doing a lot of things right, which any of the Europeans are doing wrong. Unfortunately, as Putin has said, many of the problems of the United States stem from opposition to Trump, not only to the U.S. relationship with Russia being improved, but to Trump being blocked from implementing his campaign promises to reverse the destruction of the U.S. economy.

The momentum right now is with Asia, and this is why the Schiller Institute is insisting that the United States and the European nations should ally with the Asian countries to overcome poverty, develop the globe, have win-win cooperation of all nations in this world, and build a new community for the shared future of humanity. I think this is so much within reach, that if people just knew about this New Paradigm that is emerging so very, very quickly, they would become optimistic right away! It is only the lack of knowledge of what is going on in these parts of the world that is the cause for pessimism, and why so many people see no way to change it.

I think Zanni is right—the European Parliamentarian you just quoted—change is possible. And that is really a very, very optimistic message. So join the Schiller Institute and be part of it!

**Schlanger:** To conclude, Helga, I want to bring up something I'm sure is very dear to your heart, which was the launching of a rocket from Russia to take three astronauts—a Russian, an American, and a German—to the International Space Station. U.S. Ambassador Huntsman was there for the launch. And let me underscore, one of the astronauts was from Germany! What are your thoughts on this?

**Zepp-LaRouche:** Yes, that is the best news I can report about Germany. Alexander Gerst will be the new commander of the ISS [International Space Station] for half a year, and it's wonderful. It's his second space mission, and he has given many interviews. He was on the Second Channel of German TV on Sunday. In a very cheerful and actually lovable way, he described the importance of space travel and how it benefits everyone on Earth, how it serves man's curiosity to learn more about the laws of the universe. It is definitely one of the most optimistic activities we Germans can do, because this is one area where our identity as Germans, as poets, thinkers, and inventors, comes alive in stark contrast with the present political leadership or the anti-progress green outlook of all the parties in the parliament.

I think the role of space travel and exploration in uniting nations is really going to be absolutely crucial. If people can work together on the planet Earth, like the astronauts do in space—where they don't have barriers, they don't have quarrels, they work together in a task-oriented way; they explore new worlds—I think that is

*Alexander Gerst, German European Space Agency astronaut and geophysicist. He is the first of ESA's class of 2009 astronauts who has been sent into space for a second time, launching on Soyuz MS-09 June 6 together with NASA astronaut Serena Auñón-Chancellor and Russian cosmonaut Sergei Prokopyev, to the International Space Station, where he will function as its Commander.*

the future of humanity. Space science inspires many young people to know that we have not reached the end of history, that there are good reasons to develop themselves, to study, to become scientists, to start to think scientifically, or artistically as Classical artists, or poets or thinkers. This is the way for me to go. The future will belong to people who are either scientists, natural scientists, or who are artists in the tradition of the Classical cultures around the planet. It will be a more human world in which we can go forward. If you want to be part of it, to create it, to shape it, please contact us, and work with us.

**Schlanger:** And, if you haven't done so already, I encourage everyone to read the book written by your husband, Lyndon LaRouche, *Earth's Next Fifty Years*, where he laid out these challenges. And we're now about twenty years into the period in which he talked about, and many of the things which he said would have to happen are now on the verge of occurring. So we can shape this next fifty years from here, but it's going to continue to need the Schiller Institute providing a lot of the direction and the ideas for it.

Helga, thanks for joining us again, and we'll be back next week with the international webcast from the Schiller Institute.

**Zepp-LaRouche:** Yes, till next week.

APRIL 28, 1999

# The Economics 'I.Q.' Test

by Lyndon H. LaRouche, Jr.

If anyone tells you that a rising Dow-Jones stock-market index proves that the U.S. economy is growing, your reply ought to be: "Oh, you mean that the cancer is growing. Tell me, Doctor: How is the patient doing?"

Given the present circumstances of the people of most of today's world, that is not a cruel thing to say. It is something which any intelligent and honest person would consider it necessary to say under the rapidly worsening real-economic conditions in the U.S.A. today. As a report included in this *EIR Special Feature* summarizes the fact:

> During the coming six months, more U.S. citizens, especially the poor and the elderly, will die of the worsening economic sicknesses caused by current Federal Reserve Board Chairman Alan Greenspan and related *Wall Street Journal* policies, than of illnesses such as heart disease and cancer. Indeed, many of the preventable deaths from heart disease and cancer are the result of those financial and related budgetary policies.

That is simply an actuarial fact; it is not the kind of deliberately misleading index which so many foolish Americans quote so triumphantly from the large-circulation mass-media. The present trends in U.S.A. general welfare policies, especially those of Wall Street's carpetbagging HMO and related pilfering of health-care standards, are notable in this connection. No decent person would argue, that the present U.S. economy, which successfully increases the sickness and death rates of its people, especially among its elderly and poor, is a healthy economy.

The best way to understand what is happening to the stock markets, and to the personal financial accounts of many among you, right now, is to compare the present trends in financial markets since Spring 1997 with the rise in prices, measured in Reichsmarks, during the first eight months of 1923—up to the time of the Hitler's "beer-hall *Putsch*" which launched Adolf Hitler's growing influence in Germany's politics [**Figures 1A-C**]. Look at the way the personal financial savings of the German "middle class" were wiped out by the Weimar hyperinflation of 1923, and the way in which Federal Reserve Chairman Alan Greenspan's even more lunatic hyperinflationary bubble is now threatening to wipe out much or all of what you presently believe are your personal assets.

Ask yourself: Even after the world's experience with the results of that 1923 Weimar hyperinflation, why are so many politically influential and other Americans victims of the widespread superstition, that the health of an economy can be measured in prices of stocks and bonds? Why do most adult Americans today become suddenly either stupid or even plunge into episodes of wild-eyed babbling, when the subject turns to economics and economic policy? There are many contributing factors behind such behavior.

In this Special Feature, we shall consider a few typical factors, and then turn our attention to today's principal subject: How does a sane citizen determine whether an economy is actually growing, or not? Why is my standard for measuring economic health, my so-called "Triple Curve," the only effective yardstick for measuring how well, or how badly Wall Street is performing today?

## 1. The Idea of the 'Triple Curve'

The simple fact of the existence of inflation, ought to be accepted as a warning, that the total price of commodities in a financial market, can grow, even rapidly, under the condition that the net physical output of the same economy is shrinking. Therefore, all sane adults *should* consider it a childish superstition, to suggest that the index of prices in financial markets, such as the typical Wall Street

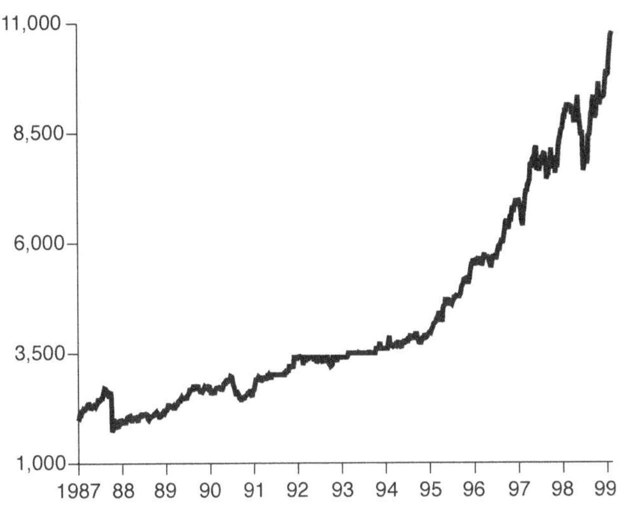



Source: Dow Jones.



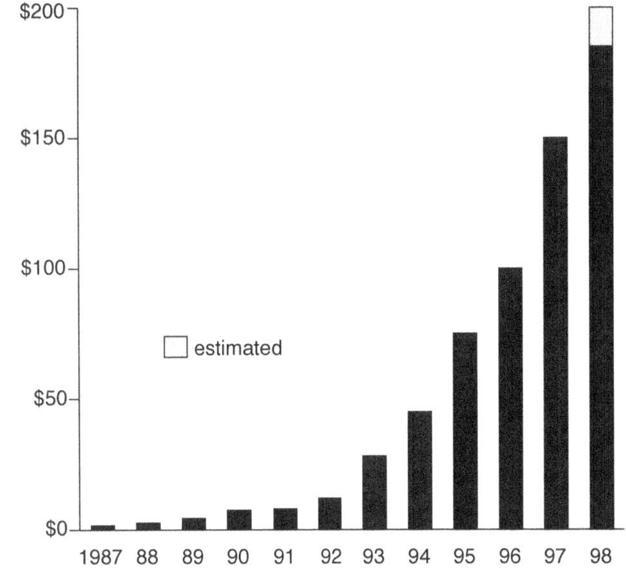



Source: *EIR*.



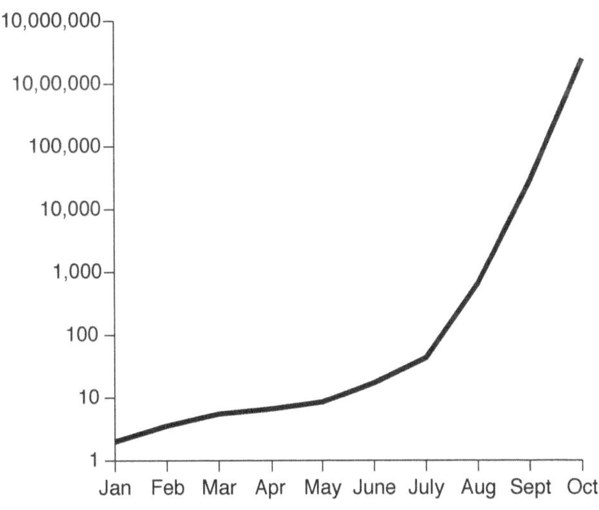



Source: *Zahlen zur Geldentwertung in Deutschland 1914 bis 1923*.

indexes, can be used as a measure of the performance of the real economy associated with those markets.

As I shall also show here, a related cautionary observation must be applied to terms such as "national income," or in using other such simple-minded notions of monetary turnover as a measure of "economic growth."

Similarly, the use of "financial futures" contracts, such as so-called "derivatives," as a method of so-called "hedging against financial risk," is a form of pure gambling, which no one should attempt to dignify with a term such as "investments."

Since the Trilateral Commission's U.S. Carter Administration, under whose direction the presently chronic Federal budgetary deficit was first generated by structural changes introduced into the U.S. economy, there has been an accelerating shift in the functional composition of so-called U.S. national income.[1] An ever-smaller

portion of total nominal national income (and of so-called Gross National Product) has represented actual output of produced goods and production-related services, while there has been an accelerated growth in purely parasitical, fictitious financial wealth. Today's fictitious wealth features prominently nominal income related to traffic in "junk bonds" and so-called "financial

---

1. Don't quibble. Admittedly, the present downward trend in the net physical performance of the U.S. economy has remained irreversible since the 1971-1972 beginning of the presently continuing shift of the IMF into a "floating exchange-rate monetary system." Admittedly, the 1971 collapse of the U.S. dollar was set into motion with the beginning of the shift to a post-industrial society, with policy-changes introduced during 1967-1968. However, the structural demolition of the U.S. economy began in earnest with the package of policies which the Trilateral Commission-created Carter Administration adopted from the New York Council on Foreign Relations' (CFR's) 1975-1976 *Project for the 1980s* (New York: Magraw-Hill, 1977), a report co-supervised by Carter Secretary of State Cyrus Vance and Carter National Security Advisor Zbigniew Brzezinski. It was the structural reforms which Carter adopted from that report, which have been the continuing cause of the presently chronic Federal debt-crunch.

derivatives." Today, it is not the U.S. economy which has been growing; it is only the cancer which is growing, while it, the disease, sucks the life out of the patient.

Under the conditions which have prevailed increasingly, inside the U.S.A., since the shock-wave effects of the 1979-1982 implementation of former U.S. Federal Reserve Chairman Paul Volcker's Trilateralist monetary policies, the standards formerly used to measure U.S. Gross National Product (GNP) no longer work with even the approximate usefulness they continued to offer up until middle to late 1983. Most of what is shown as national income today, includes categories of purely nominal wealth which virtually did not exist prior to 1971, many of which were rightly considered illegal prior to radical changes in law introduced under Kemp-Roth and like-minded propositions. In short, most of this category of nominal income is purely fictitious: you would not try to feed your children with it, and should have the decency not to wish to be seen wearing it in public.

The question is: Since neither financial market indexes, nor "Gross National Product" are any longer even approximately meaningful measures of performance of the national economy, what measurements should be used instead? This Special Feature defines and explains those needed measurements.

Any modern economy, including both the U.S. economy and what were called "states with socialist constitutions," such as the former Soviet Union, can be described in terms of the interrelationship among three variable magnitudes. These three magnitudes, which I refer to hereafter as aggregates, are: a) total money in circulation, for which the most useful estimate is what current U.S. practice names "M3"; b) financial aggregates: outstanding claims for present and future payment, both explicitly stated and otherwise implied; c) physical-economic aggregates: the physical-economic input and output of the economy considered as a functionally indivisible whole, even if some of that physical-economic aggregate is counted in money-prices, and some not.

To understand how a modern economy functions, we must measure the relative growth, or shrinkage of all three of these aggregates taken into account *simultaneously*. We must think of these three magnitudes as variables, in the sense mathematical physics defines variables. We must think of the interaction among the changes in these variables as defining a function. It is that function, so defined, which provides the only rea-

sonably sane and accurate measure of the relative increase or worsening of the health of the economy considered as a whole.

The saying goes: "Keep your eye on the ball!" That means that you should not allow yourself to be fooled by the fact that purchases and sales of much of the nation's physical-economic output are measured in money-prices. Just as in eating purchased food, it is not the money-price of that food which determines the effect of eating the food upon the person who eats. Never be fooled, as all too many ill-educated economists and members of Congress are, into assuming that the physical relations between production and consumption are determined by the relations among the prices paid for these physical products. Apples and nuts-and-bolts often have money-prices tagged to such objects; but, never assume, as most present-day economists do, that the mere price of nuts-and-bolts causes apples to grow.

Think of markets as nothing more than places where the property-titles to various real or purely fictitious objects are exchanged. The practical question, is how the flow of exchanges in such property-titles affects the way in which the physical economy functions. The relations between prices of property-titles and the physical-economic process are between entirely different processes. For example, in the language of the qualified mathematical physicist: Relations among money-prices are intrinsically *linear*; whereas, physical-economic processes are intrinsically *non-linear*.[2] The object of managing a financial and monetary system, is to force the financial system to behave in such an either explicitly or implicitly regulated way, as to force the flow of credit and purchasing power to be channeled in such a way as to encourage the physical economy to grow.

It is not how much fertilizer and seed one owns which caused agricultural growth; it must be put into the soil with a certain skill, otherwise nothing good will grow out of it. It is the physical way in which those materials are applied, by the farmers, to the process of production, which generates the useful output. The object is to ensure that the farmer knows what he is doing, and that that farmer is able to secure and apply the necesssary components of physical production, in the right physical way, at the appropriate physical time.

Thus, the economist, if he or she is competent, is oc-

---

2. I shall explain the absolutely decisive significance of this difference below.

## A Typical Collapse Function

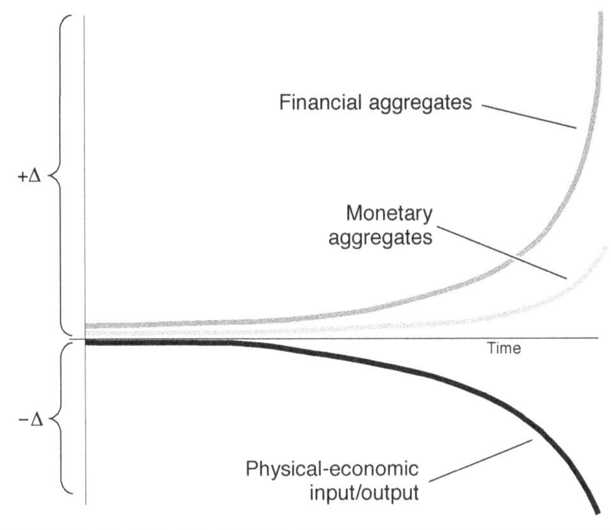


cupied with two separate issues. He ought to be concerned, primarily, with the purely physical-economic side of the economic process, without considering money or money-prices. On the money side, he must be concerned to define *physically-economically appropriate* rules for regulating trade and other financial and monetary events. The object of this regulation is to foster, preferentially, those exchanges and investments which will position the physical goods required in the place where their presence tends to produce the best physical-economic result.

If the physical economy is nonetheless functioning well, no sane person would be frightened by a fall in prices of financial investments.[3] A sane economist worries about prices of financial paper, only when falls in financial markets, or, directly opposite, hyper-inflationary expansion of what might become known soon as Wall Street's "Davey Jones" index, *cause* human suffering or collapse in technologically progressive industrial employment. After all, money has no intrinsically real economic value: "It's only paper!"

The accompanying **Figure 2**, which I introduced to

public use during the last quarter of 1995,[4] is only one example of the kinds of patterns which the functional relations among the three aggregates may describe under varying conditions. The figure shown here, represents the pattern of functional changes which have occurred within both the U.S. and most of the world's economy, over the period from about 1966 to the present date.

The principal difference between the functional relations shown by this Figure, and that of the U.S. economy in happier times, is that 1966-1967 is approximately the date at which the net growth of the U.S.A.'s physical-economy "zeroed out," the point at which investment in expansion and improvement of physical production first fell below the amount needed to sustain *future* long-term physical-economic levels of increase of productivity per-capita and per-square-kilometer, at current or better rates.

Although the physical-economic output of the economy (including military expenditures) continued to expand throughout most of the decade, this growth of output was partly the result of "burning up" earlier accumulations of capital (i.e., "savings") invested in productivity and basic economic infrastructure. With the shifts in Federal economic policy during 1966-1967, the rate of net real economic growth per capita began to decline, a decline which came to the surface during the early through middle 1970s.

Thus, approximately the middle to late 1960s, the managers of the U.S. economy abandoned their moral responsibility to maintain, deep into the future, at least the same rate of net physical-economic growth reached under the Kennedy post-Eisenhower recovery of 1962-1963.[5]

In a few moments I shall begin to explain the factors on which my retrospective dating to 1966-1967 was based. First, I shall now describe how the Figure, shown again here, was constructed.

I focus your attention on the extreme left side of the

---

3. If the U.S. were still a well-managed economy, which, admittedly, it has not been for more than a quarter-century, then, if General Motors is a profitable, well-managed firm, what conservative stockholder—"in for the long haul"—would be shaken by a drop in the price of the stock on secondary markets for financial paper? In saner times, serious investors bought into a medium- to long-term enterprise, or a long-term U.S. government bond; in a sane financial market, investors do not trade company stocks like baseball cards.

4. Lyndon H. LaRouche, Jr. (Dec. 2-3, 1995, conference address): "We Are at the End of an Epoch," *Executive Intelligence Review*, Jan. 1, 1996.

5. The use of the future as a measure of the present, applies to successive generations of national economy, as this is typified by the role of the birth, nurture, and education of those children and adolescents, who will be the performing adults of the future. I shall deal, below, with some of the deeper practical implications of this notion of the "horizon" of the future, as the measure of the economy of the present. As I explain below, no sane economist would ever suggest that any real economy can be represented in the mathematical form of a "zero-sum game."

Figure, where the horizontal and vertical, linear coordinates meet. That point corresponds to the point, 1966-1967, when some important changes in U.S. policy were introduced, including savage cut-backs from the Kennedy level of the aerospace "crash program," a program which, even to the present date, has continued to give the U.S. economy the most important factors of now vanishing, physical-economic growth of productivity since 1963.[6]

Let your eye follow the horizontal date-line across to the right side of the figure. We reach the range designated as the 1997-1999 interval, the point an encounter with an economic shock-wave effect spins the world economy into the terminal phase of the present global financial bubble.

This is the region in which the top curve, representing financial aggregates, soars to present global levels, which some leading international bankers have put at $300 trillions equivalent in unpayable financial obligations, while the physical output-levels per capita plummet steeply downward. This is the area, toward the right side of the Figure, where the financial curve zooms upward, almost vertically, while the physical-economic curve plunges more steeply downward.

This 1997-1999 interval, is an area of phase-change in the U.S.A. and world economies, the phase in which, as during mid-October 1998, G-7 central bankers, such as Federal Reserve Chairman Alan Greenspan, went baloony, and unleashed history's greatest, most insane global hyperinflationary monetary-financial bubble.

The relationship between the three curves shown on the chart, is defined in the following way.

Notice that the three curves overlap at the beginning, back in 1966-1967. Why do I use a scale at which this coincidence of the three curves appears in the chart in this way?

The problem here, is that to understand the current world economy as a process, we must compare "the prices of apples with the price-tags attached to nuts and bolts." As I stressed a few minutes ago, on the one side, we have physical-economic magnitudes, which can not be measured in money; on the other side we have financial magnitudes, such as the prices currently assigned to physical-economic magnitudes. The physical-economic magnitudes themselves are *often, but not always*

measured by markets in current money-prices. To deal with this challenge of comparing apples with price-stickers, we are obliged to introduce certain kinds of indexing. Thus, by aid of indexing, we compare a "basket" of non-monetary values, physical values, with the market-price tagged onto the contents of that "basket."

Most professional economists do this; the problem which most economists have yet to master, is how to do it in the right way.[7] Nonetheless, as most of those economists do, we construct our chart by adopting a price-index, setting the actual relations among the three aggregates—the nominal, tagged price of physical-economic aggregate, the price of monetary aggregate, and the price of financial aggregate—at a common relative value of "100" for the point 1966-1967. We then compare each of the magnitudes, separately, during each subsequent year, with the magnitude as measured at the index-year.

If we "average" the cumulative effect of trends over five to ten year intervals (so-called "running averages"), during the course of 1966-1999, the result converges upon the form shown by Figure 2. The Figure echoes the statistical fact, that there has been an accelerating relative increase of financial aggregates, a more slowly accelerating rate of increase of monetary aggregates, and a long-term rate of decline of physical-economic output per-capita and per-square-kilometer of about 2%, or more, per annum (net), until a sudden acceleration of the rate of decline since 1987-1992 (When James Carville emitted his celebrated comment on the 1992 election-campaign: "It's the economy, stupid!").

The evidence is clear. Why it has worked out that way, is not generally understood among politicians and economists, as among most citizens. That is the problem we are exposing here.

Most economists with a decent university education in mathematics, should be able to describe the way in which the recently cancerous growth of monetary and financial aggregates has occurred; even a college graduate's level of education in mathematics should be sufficient for that purpose. It is the physical-economic process—my professional speciality—which represents the critically challenging proposition, the part of the whole process which today's university economics departments, and elected members of the U.S. Congress,

---

6. Marsha Freeman, "Space Program Paid for Itself Many Times Over" (which included reference to a 1976 Chase Econometrics study), ***Executive Intelligence Review***, Feb. 23, 1996.

7. In the appropriate place below, I elaborate some of the deeper implications of indexing of "baskets of commodities."

fail, more or less miserably, to grasp. What nearly all present economists fail to grasp, is the physical-economic realities which underlie the statistics on the surface.

Here, we shall begin our outline of the interrelations among physical-economic and monetary aggregates by examining the crucial difference between two notions of financial profit: financial profit as it appears in healthy economies, and a cancer-like caricature of normal financial profit, a "bubble economy" such as that of the U.S.A. today.

## 1.1 Ordinary Financial Profit

The common-sense definition of financial profit, is something "skimmed off the top" of current output. If this amount "skimmed off the top," leaves enough of the total income behind, to keep the physical-economic costs of the real economy fully funded, we may consider the "skim" as corresponding, more or less, to ordinary financial profit.

However, the U.S. economy as a whole has not generated a net ordinary financial profit during the past twenty-five years, or slightly longer. If we take into account long-term operating costs of the real economy, such as maintaining improvements in basic economic infrastructure, and the costs of supporting a population with the same, or better demographic characteristics than when John F. Kennedy was President, and if we take into account what the U.S.A. economy's Wall Street bankers have literally stolen from parts of the world such as Central and South America, the U.S. economy as a whole has not actually *earned* a net ordinary financial profit since the "floating exchange-rate monetary system" was introduced, in 1971-1972, certainly not since Jimmy Carter was elected President. We have been living, more and more, off either looting of other countries, or from using up past savings, such as former U.S. improvements in basic economic infrastructure, since more than thirty years ago.

That is a very bad habit for any economy to acquire. It is a habit which most of our presently living citizens, unfortunately, have grown accustomed to, during more than thirty years. Without fear of exaggerating, we may say that most Americans living today, have never known the habits of a healthy form of national economy during the entirety of their adult lives. One should not be surprised that a majority of adult Americans under fifty years of age, simply don't know any better than to do the foolish things most of them have been doing during the recent decades. They never learned those habits of a sane economic life which most of us of older generations more or less took for granted, especially after the painful experience of the 1930s Depression.

In other words, today's financial profit is coming out of the physical-economic flesh and bone upon which the economy depends to continue to survive. As a result of this pattern, as Figure 2 reflects this, the per-capita and per-square-kilometer real output of the U.S. economy has been shrinking at a constant or accelerating rate, during more than a quarter-century. Yet, during the same period, the money-supply has grown impressively, and the financial aggregate has skyrocketted. Why are financial profits on Wall Street continuing to zoom?

That brings us to the matter of the bubble economy—otherwise known as an economy which we might presume is under the control of bubble-minded critters such as Federal Reserve Chairman Alan Greenspan.

Go back to the days a much saner U.S. was under the economic leadership of U.S. Treasury Secretary Alexander Hamilton. *Whenever we, as a nation, follow the principles associated with our original Federal Constitution, the authority to create currency is a natural-law monopoly of our Federal government, a Federal action taken by consent of the U.S. Congress: that is the way it should be, once again, today.*

In addition to this currency, it is permissible, and useful to generate additional monetary aggregate, not as currency, but as credit, issued through banks in much the way Germany's post-World War II *Kreditanstalt für Wiederaufbau* functioned, generating the most successful economic reconstruction program of the post-war decades, the so-called "German economic miracle."

That is, if the real economy is expanding, we need not limit credit-expansion to direct use of national currency emission plus deposited savings; we may also turn the real growth—*if it is real growth, not Wall Street's all-too-typical financial hot air*—of enterprises into an added source of *thus-secured* bank credit, issued for those kinds of loans which will foster high rates of gains in output and in per-capita productivity. That is what the *Kreditanstalt für Wiederaufbau* did, which is what the post-war economic reconstruction of Germany was, in contrast to the relatively pitiful performance of the more heavily U.S.-subsidized British and French economies during the same period.

Thus, contrary to mental cripples such as the wild-

*Former Federal Reserve Chairman Paul Volcker (left) and his Trilateralist monetary policies accelerated U.S. economic decline. U.S. Treasury Secretary Alexander Hamilton (right): "Whenever we, as a nation, follow the principles associated with our original Federal Constitution, the authority to create currency is a natural-law monopoly of our Federal government, a Federal action taken by consent of the U.S. Congress: that is the way it should be, once again, today," writes LaRouche.*

EIRNS/Stuart Lewis

eyed followers of Professor Milton Friedman, increase of the money-supply is not naturally inflationary. It all depends how the credit flows. If the combination of expanded currency and credit flows into increase of the productivity of the physical-economy, per capita and per square kilometer, the credit expansion must continue or even be expanded in rate. In that case, the result will tend to be deflationary, not inflationary. Better quality of products and increased productivity are inherently deflationary, in the real-economy sense of deflationary. Credit-expansion is inflationary, when the result is the increase of rates of financial turnover exceeding the rate of combined real physical-economic output.[8]

However, there is another way to generate financial profit: the sick way. This means the kind of profit earned by a gambling house, the Seventeenth-Century Tulip bubble, the early Eighteenth-Century John Law-style financial bubbles, or today's greatest of all bubbles, history's most lunatic bubble of them all, the Alan Greenspan bubble. Most of the growth of total U.S. financial aggregate since approximately the time of the bubble-headed Garn-St Germain and Kemp-Roth legislation, represents a purely fictitious form of wealth, a John Law-style "bubble economy."

Garn-St Germain, piled on top of the lunatic deregulation binge launched by the Trilateral Carter Administration, destroyed much of the essential structure of regulation upon which the post-Hoover U.S. recovery from Andrew Mellon's Great Depression depended. Carter's Federal Reserve Chairman, Paul Volcker, bankrupted the savings and loan banks (among other things), and Garn-St Germain set up the previously illegal way in which "junk bond" and similar Wall Street forms of piracy, looted the hulks of the ruined savings-and-loan industry.

Kemp-Roth proves how stubborn, opportunistically minded dunderheads such as Polyconic's Jude Wanniski, a key figure of the Jack Kemp roster, can become. In earlier, saner times, the U.S. government created highly successful tax-incentives for productive investments in capital improvements, such as the Kennedy era's investment-tax-credit program. Kemp-Roth did the direct opposite, drawing the money out of investment in productive capital, and pouring it into what became the gigantic financial cancer of today, that super-leveraged, $300 trillions-scale financial bubble

---

8. Provided that the increases in capital-intensity of productive investment represent investment in scientific and technological progress, useful basic economic infrastructure, or investments in social infrastructure of future economic growth, such as an improved, expanded educational program, or social-welfare system, the diversion of physical-economic output into these investments is countable as part of the current net output.

which has brought the world to the brink of a world-wide financial meltdown.

The purpose of a well-defined investment-tax-credit policy, is to draw spending away from wasteful, or marginally beneficial disbursements of corporate and related funds, into channelling capital funds into areas of physical-economic investment which contribute to the highest rates of gains in per-capita productivity of labor. Such programs will increase tomorrow's gross tax revenues of the nation through growth, even though the means used to foster this growth is reduction of the benefitted taxpayer's obligation today.

Kemp-Roth, with its silly "Laffer Curve," did the opposite. It cut the tax-rates on financial capital gains, thus reducing Federal tax revenues (thus inflating the Federal debt to levels way beyond those achieved by the Carter Administration's deregulation binge), while also drawing capital away from the very kinds of investments, which the former investment-tax-credit programs had so successfully fostered. A smart tax policy hits wasteful luxury, and other forms of sin, with high rates, in order to foster rewards of lower rates for the more creative and prudent investors.

What, then, is the difference between what I have

---

# 'Greenspan Vectors' Worse than Disease

For decades, the leading causes of death in the United States (and other industrialized nations) were, in order, heart disease and cancer. As of 1996, the two combined accounted for 1.275 million deaths annually in the 267 million population, out of a total death toll that year of 2.322 million. There were 733,800 deaths from heart disease, and 544,300 deaths from malignant neoplasms of all types.

However, the continuing the economic policies of the Alan Greenspan-*Wall Street Journal* approach, is creating conditions for increasing illness and death rates of all kinds, at such a pace as to *exceed* the current annual toll of heart disease and cancer.

The increasing morbidity and mortality numbers occur across a range of many differing diseases, locations, and sub-groupings in the population, but the patterns all show how the "Greenspan vectors" of worsening economic conditions are directly the cause, and the vital statistics prove it.

### Spreading poverty

First, consider generally the health implications of increasing impoverishment and lack of medical care for millions of Americans. Even by the official—that is, understated—categorization of who lives in poverty, 13.3%, or 35.8 million Americans, do as of 1997. This figure was about 12% in 1975, and it has worsened steadily. Of all American children under the age of six, an estimated 23%, or 5.5 million, live in poverty.

Along with this, the number and percentage of Americans lacking any health insurance is rising. About one-half of the full-time working poor and nearly one-third of all poor people were uninsured in 1997. That year, an estimated 43.4 million Americans, or 16.1% overall, had no health insurance coverage. This category has increased each year since 1987, when 12.9% of Americans, or 31 million, were not covered. Those most likely to lack coverage are young adults between the ages of 18 and 24, Hispanic-Americans (35% uninsured), the less educated, part-time workers, and the foreign-born.

Look at Texas, the gateway to the North American Free Trade Agreement-generated *maquiladoras.* Of all young people up to age 18, some 27%, or 1.502 million, are poor, and almost all of these lack any medical coverage.

### Managed care kills

Then, consider the "Greenspan vector" effect on those officially covered by health insurance. Most Americans now are under "managed care" or health maintenance organization (HMO) programs, directly or indirectly, and are facing *denied* or *delayed* medical treatment, to the point of increased incidence of illness and deaths among whole categories of people— the disabled, elderly, mental health patients, dialysis cases, and so on.

This trend is even more pronounced, as many HMOs go bankrupt (having lived out the lifespan of the mode of financial gouging they could maintain— limiting care, underpaying care-providers, and charging higher premiums, in order to pay high private profits). There are widespread situations like that of New Jersey's HIP program, which went bankrupt in 1998, leaving its 200,000 clients scrambling to buy

---

described here as "ordinary financial profit" and purely fictitious gains such as those tied up in the $300 trillions-sized global financial bubble of today? How do we define this difference in functional terms?

## 1.2 The Bubble Economy

Joe contracts with loan-shark Bill, to pay Bill $100 a week in perpetuity. For what amount can Bill sell that contract on some Wall Street or like-minded market? Allowing for expenses which Bill incurs, such as sending thugs to beat up Joe occasionally, how much is Bill "netting" out of the $5,200 a year?

Someone asks,"How much did Bill pay to Joe to create Joe's debt to Bill?" The question is irrelevant. Assume he paid him nothing, but either broke Joe's arm, or threatened Joe's children at the schoolyard: typical of the spirit of the tricks Wall Street has played upon the nations of Central and South America, or George Soros has played in Southeast Asia, for example. Whether Bill paid anything, or nothing, to Joe for the contract, is virtually irrelevant to assessment of the market-value of the contract on the relevant Wall Street market. Meyer Lansky's mobsters called it "vigorish;" Wall Street calls it "financial leverage."

---

their own drugs, and provide treatment, including everything from chemotherapy to hospital linens.

### Social breakdown, disease break-out

Consider the illness and death rate situation by certain specific diseases, locations, and groupings. Look at a few basic, vital statistics of the United States as of the mid-1990s.

For young black men (age 15 to 24), the death rates (deaths per 100,000 of the total population within the group) are the following: 157.6 for "homicide and legal interventions," 20.6 for suicide, 6.8 for heart disease, and 5.4 for cancers.

For infant mortality (deaths per 1,000 live births of the specified group or location) the rate of death in, for example, Washington, D.C., is 19.6, in contrast to around 5 deaths per 1,000 in 1995 in Germany, France, Scandinavia, Australia, and many other countries.

Tuberculosis rates are rising, in particular for the homeless, including the incidence of "primary TB," i.e., newly acquired, not merely reactivated TB.

For Hispanic U.S. children, rates of morbidity are running needlessly high for whooping cough (pertussis), measles, and other preventable childhood diseases, as the Hispanic population has the highest percentage (37%) of families uncovered by any health insurance. In Denver, California, Texas, and similar locations, a major public health threat of contagions is now present.

In California, 1.7 million children go without health insurance. In some areas of Los Angeles, only 30% of pre-school youngsters have been immunized. In Orange County, California, 37,000 youngsters have no immunization at all. The families are in fear that seeking health care will jeopardize their immigration status. In one *colonia* in El Paso, Texas, 25% of all children under age seven had hepatitis A.

Specifically, the 1996 Welfare Reform Act contravened the standing 1960s Medicaid law (health care for the poor), and ordered legal immigrants to wait five years before being eligible. Whole epidemics and permanent disabilities are now traceable to this law and way of thinking.

Add to this short list, the prevalence of HIV, hepatitis C, and other public health threats, and the menace of continuing Greenspan-*Wall Street Journal* economics is clear.—*Marcia Merry Baker*

TABLE 1

## Official Poverty in the United States, 1975-97

|  | Population (millions) | Number in poverty (millions) | Percent of total population |
|---|---|---|---|
| 1975 | 210.9 | 25.9 | 12.3 |
| 1980 | 225.0 | 29.3 | 13.0 |
| 1985 | 236.6 | 33.1 | 14.0 |
| 1990 | 248.6 | 33.6 | 13.5 |
| 1995 | 263.7 | 36.4 | 13.8 |
| 1997 | 267.5 | 35.8 | 13.3 |

Source: U.S. Department of Commerce, Bureau of the Census

TABLE 2

## Americans without Health Insurance, 1987-97

|  | Americans without insurance (millions) | Percent of total population |
|---|---|---|
| 1987 | 31.026 | 12.9 |
| 1990 | 34.719 | 13.9 |
| 1993 | 39.713 | 15.3 |
| 1995 | 40.582 | 15.4 |
| 1996 | 41.716 | 15.6 |
| 1997 | 43.448 | 16.1 |

Source: U.S. Deptartment of Commerce, Bureau of the Census

If the going rate for discounting such vigorish contracts were based on currently demanded yield of 20% per year, then Joe's contract to pay Bill would seek a market-price "worth" five times the expected perpetual annual income to be paid to the holder of the contract: as much as $26,000. In short, the "price-earnings" ratio at work. That would represent an amount approaching $26,000 of nominal financial capital, generated out of the "hot air" expansion of the indicated $5,200 annual yield.

The same "price-earnings ratio" magic applies to the case of gambling debts, or, the same thing, those exotic futures contracts called "financial derivatives." You don't believe it? Study the Black-Scholes formula which was used by the investors in Long Term Capital Management (LTCM) to dig an estimated $3 trillions hole in the accounts of the bankers investing in LTCM. The same magic applies to the case of the purely fictitious capital assets associated with the "junk bond" swindle. Virtually the entirety of the recent rise of the Dow-Jones index, especially since mid-October 1998, has been purely fictitious financial-capital gains, obtained as the result of exactly this sort of "price-earnings ratio" swindle.

In the case of the current Dow-Jones stock-market swindle, there are three driving factors generating that so-called "economic recovery"—"recovery" in the sense of the day the man on LSD sees "the dead rise to walk again." The first, and most important, is pure and simple insanity, sometimes also called "irrational exuberance" or "mass hysteria." The second factor is hyperinflationary monetary pumping-up of the financial bubble by culpable agencies such as Alan Greenspan's Federal Reserve System. The third is the counting of purely fictitious financial capital gains—so-called "bookkeeping profits" on today's market-index upswing—as an income-flow.

In the wild orgy of today's "economic boom on Wall Street," a huge mass of purely fictitious income-flows—"indexed bookkeeping profits on trading"—is capitalized in the same general way Joe's hypothetical contract is parlayed from a $5,200 annual payments item, into a $26,000 fictitious capitalization. However, for this scheme to be kept in play, an additional factor must be supplied: a highly-leveraged flow of central-banking and related monetary aggregate into the market.

Now, see how that so-called "Wall Street boom" is linked to the real economy.

Take the simplest case. In the case of the Federal Re-serve System, the leveraged flow of increased monetary aggregate is generated in two principal ways. One aspect of this is the straight printing of Federal Reserve Notes, the so-called "Keynesian multiplier" mechanism. The other aspect is the relationship of that mechanism, to the discounting of financial paper through the "Fed's" power to issue currency obligations against discounted financial assets deposited into the "Fed's" system. The discounting of virtual "toilet paper" in the system, expands the flow of apparent monetary aggregate (combined real and fictitious) on an enormous scale.

The ability of the "Fed" system to generate such swindles, is rooted in the functions of the "discount window."

The principle involved is the same as we witness in those parts of the world where poor farmers balance the family household budget by selling adolescent, or even pre-adolescent daughters into organized prostitution rings. If the farm is losing money, keep the farm afloat by selling daughters into sex-slavery. If the corporate enterprise is either operating at a loss, or lacking in income-margins needed to maintain its competitive position, they have available, through the "Fed" discount window's mechanisms, the same kind of help the farmer might secure by selling his daughter into sex-slavery. Loot the company, its employees, its pension plan, the quality of its product—or anything which comes to mind in a kindred spirit of enterprise, all to generate an increased margin of real or fictitious, discountable income-stream.

As I shall explain in a section of this report, below, that is what the U.S. has done to itself since approximately 1966-1967, and that most visibly since 1971-1972. It is the use of the financial mechanisms associated with this use of the discounting principle, to generate larger nominal income-streams than the physical-economy can tolerate, which has collapsed the per-capita and per-square-kilometer physical-economic output of the U.S. economy.

This looting of the physical-economic base, in order to puff up the financial structures, is the functional mechanism which links the collapse of the real economy of the U.S.A., to the hyperinflationary boom in the soon-doomed Wall Street bubble.

What has happened since mid-October 1998, is that Greenspan's "Fed," has been engaged in a greater rate of such hyperinflationary pump-priming than even that seen in the late phases of the 1923 Weimar hyperinflation. This bubble is either going to be shut down, or it is going to blow, globally, and soon.

The kinds of behavioral extremes to which I have referred in this illustration of the point, are peculiar to the terminal phase of the present world monetary system. Nonetheless, these have been the growing characteristic of the IMF system as a whole since the successive 1971-1972 and 1975 phases of the introduction of a global "floating exchange-rate" monetary system. The documentation of the purely fraudulent nature of all alleged sovereign debt, which Wall Street et al. have imposed upon the nations of Central and South America, as shown in the *EIR* study prepared and issued by Dennis Small et al., is the "classic" demonstration of the global swindle which the IMF monetary system represents from 1971-1972 to the present day. The same debt-swindle run against the leading nations of Central and South America, from the mid-1970s to the present, is the model for the swindle which the same IMF conducted against the states of the former Soviet Union and eastern Europe from the close of 1989 to the present. It is the same swindle which former Speaker of the House Newt Gingrich led against President Clinton's U.S. Federal budgets during most of the period 1995-1998.

Another example of the same kind of swindle, is the way in which the London petroleum marketing cartel deployed its asset, then U.S. Secretary of State Henry A. Kissinger, to arrange what became the "petro-dollar" hoax of the middle through late 1970s, the version of the swindle negotiated on behalf of the IMF system at the 1975 Rambouillet monetary summit. The "petro-dollar" swindle presaged the "junk bond" swindles of the 1982-1988 interval, which presaged the "financial derivatives" swindle of the 1990s, which presaged Alan "I am the Emperor Nero" Greenspan's version of the burning of Rome, the hyperinflationary bubble which Greenspan launched as part of his effort to bail out bankers deeply invested in busted hedge funds.

To summarize what we have considered thus far, look at Figure 2 again. The top curve reflects the growing per-capita ratio of chiefly fictitious financial aggregate required to keep the 1996-1999 version of the present financial system afloat. The lowest curve, reflects the effects of looting of the per-capita physical economic base, to generate fictitious income-streams used to inflate the financial-aggregates bubble. The growth of monetary aggregates reflects the functional relationship between the other two curves.

This brings us to the heart of the matter, the matter of physical-economic aggregates.

## 2.0 Real Economy: Man's Mastery of Nature

Mankind is the only species whose individual member is capable of willfully increasing the potential relative population-density of his species as a whole. This specific distinction is typically expressed by an individual mind's discovery of a validatable universal physical principle.

The science of physical economy, one of the branches of physical science founded by Gottfried Leibniz, focuses upon those changes in the axioms of human behavior through which mankind's power over nature, per capita and per square kilometer, is increased.

Mankind's functional relationship to the universe, is expressed for sense-perception in two general ways. It is expressed both in the improvements in increased life-expectancy, size of population, and other demographic characteristics of populations, and that population's increased physical power over the universe, in per-capita and per-square-kilometer terms. These perceptible forms of improvements in the human condition, are benefits acquired both through relevant changes in human behavior, as scientific and technological progress expresses this, and by alterations of nature in ways which are relevant to, and indispensable for the realization of the potential benefits implied in scientific and technological progress. Consider the physical-economic expression of those changes in human behavior first, and then the changes in the environment needed to sustain life at the higher demographic level scientific and technological progress imply.

The changes in human behavior (e.g., culture) are of principally three forms.

1. Validated discoveries of universal physical principle.
2. Validated discovery of technologies derived from the application of universal principles.
3. Validated discoveries of principles of Classical artistic composition and related matters of statecraft, through which the cognitive powers of individual members of society are mobilized for the successful implementation of such physical principles and technologies.

For our purposes here, I provide the following summary of the implications of what has just been said.

The primary task which the lessons of physical

economy demand of society, is the protection and the cultivation of the developed cognitive powers of each individual personality. That is to say, the task of society is not only to foster the productive activity upon which the society's existence depends, but to develop the individual's cognitive and related powers in such a way that high levels of productivity are maintained, and that further progress in this direction is ensured. Thus, on these accounts, and with that qualification, educational policies become the central determinant of the success or failure of an economy. It is from this vantage-point, that the curve of physical-economic aggregates is best understood.

## 2.1 The Function of Education

In general, the well-advised society places the greatest emphasis upon three aspects of the development of the mind of the individual. First, the quality of nurture of the pre-school-age child. Second, education and related research as such. Third, the cultural standard of relations among persons generally in the society.

In these three phases of the development of the individual mind, the central obligation of society is to foster a well-founded self-image of the individual person, as someone of a quality absolutely apart from and above the level of any other living species. This is effectively achieved through such means as the child's delight in effecting a validatable discovery of universal principle, or discoveries akin to that, through what the child is able to recognize as the creative character of the cognitive potentials of that child's mind.

This is the standpoint, for example, of the tradition of what is known as Christian humanist education. Examples of this tradition include the work of the Brothers of the Common Life, the echoes of that in the work of the Oratorians of France and Italy, and the Schiller-Humboldt Classical Humanist education program which Prussian Reformer Wilhelm von Humboldt established in Germany. Similar approaches are found in the work of the Winthrops and Mathers in the Massachusetts Bay Colony, and in the best like-minded currents of education in the pre-John Dewey U.S.A.

The object of a Classical Humanist or kindred form of educational policy, is the production of what might be termed "the cultivated mind." Look at this now from the vantage-point of physical science.

All of our knowledge of our effectively willful relations to the physical universe, rests upon an aggregation of validated universal physical principles. These principles occurred originally in the form of creative cognitive acts by individual minds. In many cases, although not in all, the names of those discoverers are known to pupils and others, as the personal name attached to the discovered principle in question. The proper object of education, is to create the circumstances, as in the classroom, in which the student replicates the actual original act of discovery.

In other words, a poor kind of school teaches a pupil to learn the name of the principle together with explanations and illustrations of its application. That latter kind of education, called "learning," tends to deaden the cognitive powers of the pupil's mind. Only by exception, could pupils abused by such mere "how to" learning, manifest later the qualities of a truly cultivated mind.

By "cultivated mind," we should agree to signify a mind which has been shaped by the process of accumulating a store of experiences of original cognitive generation of validated universal physical principles. Our job is to provide the environment, the teachers, and the opportunities, by aid of which each child and adolescent may reach adulthood with a good approximation of the qualities of a cultivated mind.

On the professional level of physical and related science, the graduate should have reenacted the original discovery of most of the known leading validated discoveries of universal physical principle, accomplished by mankind up to the present time. This is no small matter; existing scientific knowledge of principle is best represented by a Riemannian manifold of the kind Riemann himself defines in his celebrated 1854 habilitation dissertation. That graduate should have also demonstrated such mastery of principles to the extent of original work of discovery. That is the rule-of-thumb definition of a "cultivated scientific mind."

A society which has educated its young by such a cognitive standard, produces the kind of labor-force of which it might be said, "They can do anything." Instead of merely learning "how to" do this or that, they know how to solve problems lying within, or even slightly beyond the reach of the validated universal principles, whose original discovery they have reexperienced.

Such an educational policy costs. It is a major element of governmental and related budgetary outlays. Nonetheless, whatever a quality education costs—unlike that being provided currently—in the final analysis, it represents one of the most essential costs of doing business. Since about 1963, there has been a cumulatively catastrophic decline in the competence of teachers, the general quality of education, and the competence for life of the graduates of our public schools and universities.

In Germany, for example, the "Brandt Reforms" destruction of the Humboldt policy for education, has produced a young German school-leaver who is almost of a lower mental class than the members of the same family who completed their *Abitur* (secondary-school diploma), under the impact of the Humboldt legacy. One might justly suspect, that those malignant souls who influenced this disastrous reform in Germany, both from the U.S.A. and through the 1963 Paris OECD proposal, were motivated by hatred of Germany and Germans. Generally, in Europe and the U.S.A., there has been a catastrophic collapse in the cognitive skills and related qualities of potential productivity of the labor-force.

The same principle applies to education in Classical artistic composition and related aspects of statecraft. I have indicated this aspect of the matter in my ***The Road to Recovery*** and other published locations.

## 2.2 Infrastructure

When the English-speaking colonists reached Massachusetts, Virginia, Pennsylvania, and elsewhere, they found a virtual economic desert, a wilderness. Out of that wilderness, they hewed fertile farms, towns, roadways, canals, and later railroads. From an earlier time, the case of Charlemagne should remind us, that the rise of Europe from the barbarism left in the wake of the Roman Empire's collapse into a new dark age, was based largely on the same kind of attention to investment in public infrastructure. In the seemingly miraculous doubling of the prosperity of France under King Louis XI, similar kinds of measures are outstanding.

Such development of the population's land-area constitutes what our senses present to us as the basic physical infrastructure of the society. However, we should readily recognize that education as defined above, and also expressions of Classical artistic composition, are also part of the basic economic infrastructure, even though the cognitive processes which are the subject of education are not sense-perceptible phenomena in and of themselves. The development of the mind and of the perceptible nature of the nation, constitutes its basic economic infrastructure.

There is a relatively clear difference between society's expenditures to maintain and improve basic economic infrastructure, on the one hand, and for investment in production of goods on the other. The preconditions for the generally successful forms of investment in production of goods, for example, depend upon the ability to situate that production within a suitably prepared environment. That environment is the basic economic infrastructure required.

Thus, in our form of economy, as established under our original Federal Constitution, there is a division between private enterprise, and the obligation of government to provide for development of all of the population and all of the land-area, through generalized education and other forms of basic economic infrastructure. The state's development of roads, waterways, railroads, and other basic economic infrastructure either provided or regulated by government, is thus contrasted with private investment in a particular farm, manufacturing facility, and so on. It is a matter of "property," so to speak. The government is responsible for the *general welfare*, the development and protection of the quality of all of the people and all of the land-area. The authority of private investment is limited to the domain which it owns, although what may be done within that domain is limited to actions not in conflict with the general welfare.

The maintenance and improvement of matters of basic economic infrastructure, is just as much an essential capital investment as the maintenance and improvement of a farm, or an investment in a manufacturing facility. Thus, the maintenance and improvement of basic economic infrastructure at the level necessary to maintain progress, is a non-divestible cost of everything produced by that society as a whole. Under the fundamental law of the U.S. Constitution, the full maintenance and improvement of the general welfare is a non-divestible obligation, an obligation which no positive law can rightly revoke in whole or part.

One of the crucial factors which define 1971-1972 as a downward turning-point for the U.S. economy as a whole, is the fact, that combined cuts in effective wage-rates, as instituted under President Nixon's "Phase I" and "Phase II" programs, and a persisting non-maintenance of pre-existing public and related investments in basic economic infrastructure, were the sectors of the total economy in which the greatest portion of the shrinkage of the real economy was concentrated. This ruinous trend was accelerated under the Trilateral Carter Administration's savage programs of deregulation and looting of the farm sector.

Take the case of transportation.

The cheapest form of transportation, per ton, is wa-

*Left: President John Kennedy and John Glenn at Cape Canaveral, 1962. Right: President Dwight Eisenhower (right) with Queen Elizabeth and Prince Philip. "The Eisenhower government never brought useful programs to the threshold-level at which durable net economic growth-rates were reached. President Kennedy's escalation of the pre-existing U.S. space-mission program, to the level of the specified commitment to the manned Moon landing, is an example of the difference in performance between the Eisenhower and Kennedy administrations," writes LaRouche.*

terborne transport.

The most efficient modes of transportation are railways and magnetic-levitation systems—provided those mass-transit systems are not mismanaged. Relatively more costly, and less efficient, are highway vehicles. From the standpoint of the population in general, and also employers and their employees, one of the most important sources of economic waste is the time lost in commuting, and increased costs incurred by the society to support systems of commuting more than short times and relatively short distances. The design of cities and of mass-transit systems in ways which counter the directly and indirectly incurred social and other costs of commuting, ought to be recognized as one of the leading imperatives of policies of government at the Federal, state, and local levels.

The end of net railway expansion, which was reached during the mid-1920s, was a key symptom and factor in the long-range decline in the U.S. economy, the decline leading into the 1930s Great Depression, and the post-war decline in the functional quality of our

nation's urban development. During World War II, we wisely revived the national rail system (otherwise we might have lost the war), but we proceeded to destroy that system during the 1950s and beyond. The destruction came partly through mismanagement and obsolescence of various forms, and largely through Wall Street's looting of great systems such as the New York Central and Pennsylvania systems.

Take the case of the transport of freight from the metropolitan New York region to Chicago, the two great Atlantic-oriented hubs of our nation's waterborne and land-based transport of freight. It is far cheaper to ship long-haul goods overnight from New York to Chicago by rail systems, than the inherently less efficient and more costly truck transport. However, back in the 1950s, obsolescent practices in freight handling within the truck-rail local-long-distance interface, caused the more costly truck transport to be preferred over rail. The remedy for the problem was obvious: a well-planned merger of the Pennsylvania and New York Central systems would have proffered a solution, but the Wall Street crowd vetoed the merger at that time, thus condemning both railroads to the looting, ruin, and government interventions, which inevitably ensued from failure to clean out the obsolescent practices. It was not the railways which failed; it was the ownership of the railways which ruined the railroads.

Admittedly, there was another factor in this: a factor once referred to as the national defense highway system: the illegitimate father, so to speak, of our present system of so-called "superhighways." For our purposes here, two points on this matter are sufficient.

The notion of establishing a national defense highway system, was introduced as a response to the vulnerability of national railway systems to attack by long-range bombers. The national defense highway system was intended to provide both a supplement and an alternative to the railway system, on which the logistics of the U.S. World War II mobilization had depended so much. The relevant financial high-binders soon came up with another idea: instead of a restricted access national defense highway system, a system which would open up rural areas for suburban residential and shopping-center complexes.

This orgy of real-estate speculation complemented the so-called Eisenhower consumer-credit, "Baby Boomer" bubble of the 1954-1957 interval, the financial bubble which collapsed in the 1957-1958 recession and the ensuing economic doldrums of 1959-1960.[9]

Many myths were concocted in the effort to debunk President Kennedy's 1960 electoral victory over Vice-President Richard Nixon. There were, admittedly, numerous good programs launched under President Eisenhower. The fault in those good programs of the Eisenhower period, such as the post-Sputnik revival of the previously mothballed space program, was that the Eisenhower government—sometimes called the "Eisenhowever government"—never brought useful programs to the threshold-level at which durable net economic growth-rates were reached. President Kennedy's escalation of the pre-existing U.S. space-mission program, to the level of the specified commitment to the manned Moon landing, is an example of the difference in performance between the Eisenhower and Kennedy administrations.

To understand the roots of this difference in economic policies between the Eisenhower and Kennedy administrations, a glance at the personal history of Dwight Eisenhower is helpful.

Eisenhower's road toward high military rank was early defined by his posting as an aide to General Douglas MacArthur, an Eisenhower later wryly described by MacArthur as "the best clerk I ever had." In the course of things, Eisenhower's career veered to links with Winston Churchill-funder Bernard Baruch's Wall Street. When the time came to induce Winston Churchill et al., to submit to the indignity of having a U.S. military commander of allied forces for the war in Europe, Eisenhower was designated as acceptable to London. From that point on, to the end of his Presidency, Dwight Eisenhower was the kind of U.S. patriot whose role was to manage the difficult U.S. partnership with the always nasty British—during World War II in Europe, in the early days of NATO, and as President.[10]

The difference was, that John F. Kennedy's tendency was to model his administration upon the legacy of President Franklin Roosevelt. As Kennedy matured in office, the echoes of the patriotic legacy of Franklin Roosevelt became clearer, the youthful Romantic edges relatively more moderated. In that sense and degree, the differences between Kennedy and Eisenhower, echoed the differences between the American traditionalism of

---

9. The February-March 1957 outbreak of the 1957-1958 recession began as I had forecast some months earlier. That forecast was based upon a study of the post-1954 consumer-credit bubble, a study centered upon the John Law-like frenzy in automobile production and marketing over the course of the 1954-1956 interval. By 1956, many dealers in leading brands were losing money on new car sales, but were deluded by the industry's dealership accounting methods, into believing the losses were being incurred on account of the used-car market. The automobile manufacturers considered it in their interest to brainwash the dealers into thinking that the new-car sales were the money-makers. When new-car financing reached the level of thirty-six months, including a giant "balloon note" in the last scheduled payment, the evidence was that this bubble was about to blow. A similar state of affairs prevailed in other categories of consumer-sales financing.

10. To give a precise indication of the problems faced by Eisenhower as commander of allied forces in Europe, take the case of the wretched British Field Marshall Montgomery. Years later, I asked Professor Friedrich Freiherr von der Heydte, "Would you agree, that Montgomery was the worst commander of any nation during World War II?" The Professor chuckled: "You can't say anything bad about Montgomery to me; he saved my life. I was commanding Rommel's rearguard; if Montgomery had ever flanked me, I was dead...." From El Alamein to Market Garden, Montgomery used his position within the allied command to delay allied victory by at least six months, if not significantly more. As Britain's John Wheeler-Bennett emphasized, after the war: the British did not wish to win the war too soon. Thus, British intelligence betrayed the plotters against Hitler to the Gestapo. Thus, Eisenhower was obliged by his British partners to put up with the wretched Montgomery.

Franklin Roosevelt, and the "we must learn to work with the difficult British" vacillations of an Eisenhower.

There were signs that Kennedy was leaning more toward the statesmanship of Franklin Roosevelt, General Douglas MacArthur, President Charles de Gaulle, and Chancellor Konrad Adenauer, than what we have seen as a trend in U.S. policy-shaping since. Viewing matters from that standpoint, helps to make clearer the causes for the difference in quality of economic and related leadership, between the fumbling economic policies of the Eisenhower administration, and the bolder thrusts of the Kennedy administration.

The Eisenhower administration sometimes put its shoulder behind some good efforts, but those efforts were never bold enough to make London and its Wall Street minions seriously unhappy. Neither cold, nor hot, but lukewarm: the 1957-1958 recession is typical of the result of the Eisenhower administration's compromises with reality.

Three features of the 1961-1966 interval are outstanding examples of what had been good in the Kennedy policies, and what had turned sour beginning the 1966-1967 period of the war in Indo-China:

1. The Kennedy "crash program" for a manned Moon landing. For every penny spent on that program, the U.S. economy gained a spillover of more than ten cents in benefit. This was the largest single stimulant for the real economy since that program was launched.

2. The improved investment tax-credit program, the complement to the aerospace "crash program" in boosting the real economy.

3. The continued expansion of investment in maintenance and improvement of basic economic infrastructure, a program which was cut back to effect a continuing net contraction of U.S. infrastructure from about 1971 to the present.

Today, those beauties of the past are gone. Our nation's basic economic infrastructure is in a general state of rot. The very name of "general welfare," the pillar of our constitutional law, has been treated as if it were a "dirty word." Education is, for the greater part, worse than a bad joke; an assay of popular entertainment, exposes the nation as afflicted with a type of ruinous cultural decay best suited to Sodom and Gomorrah, or some other culture which has lost the moral fitness to survive. Investment tax-credit incentives for growth have been thrown aside, replaced by the lunatic philosophy of Kemp-Roth and Garn-St Germain. Real science, the banner of every economic triumph of our nation's past, has been turned into another "dirty word."

## 2.3 Industry and Agriculture

The pillar of modern industry was defined by Gottfried Leibniz's study of the principles of heat-powered machinery. Thus, the first operating steam-engine, used to power a river-boat, was developed in collaboration with Leibniz, in Germany, at the beginning of the Eighteenth Century. Leibniz's principles were expressed later by the work of France's Lazare Carnot, in defining the principles of machine-tool design used to ensure France's victory over invading armies, during 1792-1794. Modern industrial society was defined by the U.S. program of 1861-1876, a model based upon the principles of Carnot, which was exported during and after 1876, to Germany, Japan, Russia, and other countries.

Carnot's discovery of the elementary principles of machine-tool design was based upon Leibniz's conception of the geometry of position. The fuller appreciation of these principles lies within the bounds of the successive development of what are known as hypergeometries, as by Carl Gauss and Bernhard Riemann. It is the application of a thus-refined conception of machine-tool design, as applied to the design of unique proof-of-principle experiments, which made modern industry, and also agriculture, possible. It is on this basis, and only this basis, that the principles of modern industrial society can be understood with reasonable efficiency.

The application of any validated discovery of universal physical principle, results in the production of new technologies, presented as by-products of sundry sorts of applications of those universal principles. What we see in any successful modern machine-tool design, is a multiply-connected assembly of such technologies. What one should recognize in any industrial or related productive process as a whole, is precisely the same thing. Thus, in this way, the general theory of production is to be viewed as a generalized application of the principles of Riemannian manifolds. From this standpoint, it is possible to make sense of the economic issues posed in defining necessary costs and expenses of the productive process.

Focussing upon industry and agriculture, there are two opposing trends at work in a healthy form of modern economy. On the one side, there are increasing costs associated with the increasing (physical-economic) capital-intensity, energy density, energy-flux density, and energy-coherence of the productive process. This is a factor of increasing cost. However, increases in productivity obtained in this way reduce the per-capita combined costs of production, relative even to an associated rising capital-intensity and energy-intensity.

The imperative of increasing capital- and energy-intensities is underscored by regard to the factor of technological attrition. As we deplete what had been the cheapest and more readily available resources, even the need to keep per-capita physical-economic costs from rising, compels us to make what had been poorer resources, cheaper than richer resources earlier. We must either continue scientific and technological progress, or be plunged into ruin for failing to do so. There are additional considerations, but this is sufficient to make the point.

The same considerations show us why the machine-tool sector of the division of labor, is the driving force, the determinant of the economic success or failure of economies. This is demonstrated today, by the fact, that without a healthy German economy, there can be no healthy European economy at large. In turn, there can be no healthy German economy, unless that economy is dominated by export-oriented machine-tool production. On the other side of the scale, it would be enormously difficult to meet the challenge of economic justice for the vast populations and areas of Asia, without a massive, greatly expanded flow of the most modern machine-tool design, from the U.S.A., a Germany-centered European economy, Japan, and the machine-tool potential of the former Soviet scientific military-industrial complex.

The structure of industry (and, also modern agriculture) is therefore highly capital-intensive, and increasingly so. For the same reason, a successful modern economy is increasingly science-and-technology intensive, requiring corresponding educational and cultural standards for the populations at large.

Comparing the changes in these elements which have been induced during the recent quarter-century (and longer), we are confronted with shocking evidence of the degree we have destroyed our economy over this past period to date.

### 2.4 What Is Cost?

The true cost of production is whatever combination of ingredients is required to enable a population to sustain a specific rate of increase of the rate of growth of output, as growth is measured in terms of those ingredients.

I shall supply here some rough indications of the way in which physical-economic and money-priced aggregates are to be compared for such purposes as constructing a set of curves such as those shown in Figure 2.

This means that reliance upon "constant dollar" estimates of income and cost is irresponsible practice. It is the physical relationship between the physical-economic market-baskets representing costs, which must be compared with physical-economic productivity per capita and per square kilometer, not monetary prices, nor adjusted monetary prices. Furthermore, although the infrastructure built up twenty or more years ago is an integral part of the functional costs incurred by today's production-output, the cost of actual replacing depleted infrastructure is usually not counted at all, or is estimated in historical accounting prices, not current prices of production.

There is, in short, no competent deductive determination of the relationship between prices of items in market-baskets of costs and expenses, and output in current or adjusted prices.

Rather, the functional value of per-capita baskets of physical-economic inputs is measured in terms of relative rates of increase of the physical-economic rate of profit represented by current output. In the first approximation, the measure of the value of inputs is the rate of increase of output over input, realized through the modes of production and consumption in use. More precisely, it is the rate of increase or decrease of that rate of profit, which is closest to an exact measure of

> **For more than ninety percent of our U.S. population, the conditions of life, and levels of productivity become worse, and yet, many of the people having these sense-perceptions, speak of the "growth of the U.S. economy." Such people are like the shopper who says, "I don't worry about the farmer; I get my milk from the supermarket."**

physical-economic values.

The only meaningful determination of that rate of profit, is in both per-capita and per-square-kilometer terms. Assign all of the elements of physical-economic cost (input), including physical-capital factors, as cost of labor. Deduct the imputable replacement-costs of all of those elements of input, in prices, from total physical-economic output, combined, in current money prices.

Take an example. Since the 1946-1966 interval, the number of jobs which the average member of the family household must have, to meet the same standard of living as five or ten years earlier, has risen. In the post-1966 period, the birth-rate for most classes of households has declined. (In some parts of the world, such as Germany, catastrophically.) Add to the number of working-hours in the week so represented, the added commuting time involved. Compare the physical standard of household life, in physical-economic, not monetary terms, to earlier periods. For most of the U.S. population, the conditions of life have become steadily worse, especially since the 1987 Wall Street stock-market crash.

Look to the future: look to the children and adolescent members of those households. Look at education. For the population in general, there are virtually no competent teachers, no competent educational programs, and no decent textbooks in the public schools today. Former classrooms are being replaced by what used to be called the "blab schools" of the poorest areas of Kentucky and Tennessee, at the beginning of this passing century. The lack of time for family nurture in households, aggravates the epidemic of illiteracy among not only public-school leavers, but also university graduates.

Look at the effects of the growing functional illiteracy within the population, upon the ability of the U.S. economy to produce. Look how far behind other nations the U.S.A. has been falling on these and related accounts.

Look to the effect of Wall Street's looting of healthcare, through HMOs and kindred arrangements, and the effects of this on the families of the most targetted infirm and elderly strata of the population. Look at mortality and illness rates among infants and young children. Look at the rampaging resurgence of epidemic disease once formerly brought to near the vanishing point.

Look at the family farms which used to feed us. Look at the towns where former productive industries have long vanished under the impact of Carter's deregulation of transportation, and other disastrous structural reforms.

All of these and related physical-economic considerations, touch evidence plainly within the reach of our sense-perceptions. For more than ninety percent of our U.S. population, the conditions of life, and levels of productivity become worse, and yet, many of the people having these sense-perceptions, speak of the "growth of the U.S. economy." Such people are like the shopper who says, "I don't worry about the farmer; I get my milk from the supermarket." They have literally left their senses behind. For them, the important thing is money.

One is thus reminded of those Germans of the early 1920s, the so-called "middle class," people who owned no workshop, no farm, or other means of producing real wealth, but who had entrusted their wealth to bank savings and financial investments. Then, the 1923 Weimar hyperinflation wiped out their savings and their financial investments. Speaking of today's terrible U.S. public schools, one might say, as was said in times past, that those who do not study history, obviously will learn nothing from it.

Lyndon LaRouche's university textbook on national economic policy, which also serves as a manual for government officials and advisors to governments.

# The Economics You Need To Know To Create a Future for Mankind

June 8—Two systems are now before the world. One, the City of London/Wall Street trans-Atlantic financial empire, has been in a state of "free fall" since the 2007-2008 crash, a crash forecast by Lyndon LaRouche in a July 25, 2007 webcast, in which he said:

> What's listed as stock values and market values in the financial markets internationally is bunk! These are purely fictitious beliefs. There's no truth to it; the fakery is enormous. There is no possibility of a non-collapse of the present financial system—none! It's finished, now! The present financial system cannot continue to exist under any circumstances, under any Presidency, under any leadership, or any leadership of nations. Only a fundamental and sudden change in the world monetary financial system will prevent a general, immediate chain-reaction type of collapse. At what speed we don't know, but it will go on, and it will be unstoppable! And the longer it goes on before coming to an end, the worse things will get.

How could LaRouche forecast this?

The other system now before the world, the World Land-Bridge, better known as "the New Silk Road," and called by China and its allies in 140 nations the "Belt and Road Initiative" (BRI), is a product of the 25-year-plus collaboration of Lyndon LaRouche with China, Russia and other nations. The immediate, future upward direction of world economic progress has been outlined by LaRouche in a book entitled *Earth's Next Fifty Years*.

How can LaRouche, or anyone else, forecast the future for mankind?

Recently, the LaRouche Political Action Committee (LPAC) launched a Campaign for the Future, the three planks of which are: (1) Stop the British coup d'etat against the U.S. Presidency; (2) Implement Lyndon LaRouche's Four Laws of American System economics; and (3) Join the World Land-Bridge, a conception initiated by LaRouche in the 1990s, launched by the Chinese in the form of the One Belt, One Road policy, and now embraced by over a hundred countries.

Starting June 22, LPAC will offer an eight-part class series on the science of physical economy. Completely untaught in American universities today—despite the work of 19th century American economists Mathew and Henry Carey, Friedrich List, E. Peshine Smith and many others—physical economy is the only competent basis upon which a prosperous future for the United States, or any other country, could be established. Originally created by German scientist Gottfried Leibniz (1646-1716), and advanced by Benjamin Franklin and Alexander Hamilton among others, it was Lyndon LaRouche who achieved breakthroughs in physical economy in the 1950s that allowed him to accurately forecast, in nine different instances, crises in the financial system and the economy, all of which could have been averted. As a result of his documented success, today LaRouche's ideas are widely studied in China, Russia, and other countries.

Shouldn't these ideas be studied in the policy circles of the United States?

During and after his successful campaign for President, Donald Trump called for implementing the American System of economics, but he has done little so far to demonstrate a scientific understanding of what that means in practice. Does he have such an understanding? It is unclear. And yet a more important question is, do you know what the American System of economics is? Would you like to know all about real economics, not money? Are you ready to fight to gain that knowledge?

The bad news is: If you have taken a course in economics at a university, it is absolutely certain that you have no idea what the American System of economics is, because it is not taught in any known university. All that is taught is one form or another of British monetarism. If the instructors even mentioned physical economy, you were probably falsely told that the American System is based on the free trade policy of Adam Smith's *Wealth of Nations*—against the which, the American Revolution of George Washington and Alexander Hamilton was actually fought!

There are other traps set for every ideological taste. If you are a Republican, you have probably been brainwashed into following Milton Friedman. If you are a Democrat, you are probably a follower of John Maynard Keynes. If you are a socialist, it is a certainty that you don't know that Marxist economics is just another anti-American branch of British economics. So, how can a person escape the indoctrination that passes for education?

If you don't want to be a mere underling of the Anglo-Dutch liberal imperialist system; if you want to free the United States and the rest of the world from our historic and contemporary British enemy; if you want to be truly mentally free to shape a positive future for mankind, your only efficient choice is to get to know the work and wisdom of Lyndon LaRouche, the most successful economic forecaster in history and the only scientific proponent of the American System of economics in the world today.

In an eight-week course in LaRouche's economics, you will be challenged to question all of the accepted, but nonetheless false, axiomatic assumptions which have wreaked economic havoc on this nation and much of the rest of the world, increasingly since World War II, and which continue to be an obstacle to the creation of a New Paradigm of Global Peace based on Economic Development. More importantly, you will learn the anti-entropic scientific principles which underlie mankind's limitless future. Most importantly, by challenging and having the courage to change your own axioms, you will be challenged to make the creation of that New Paradigm the mission of your life.